Memorable
Christmas Stories

Memorable Christmas Stories

Compiled by Leon R. Hartshorn

1980

Published by Deseret Book Company, Salt Lake City, Utah 1980

First printing in paperbound edition, July 1991

Library of Congress Catalog Card No. 74-15999

ISBN 0-87579-497-1

Printed in the United States of America

10   9   8   7   6   5   4   3   2   1

Contents

I Think You Have a Fire at Your Store

LARUE H. SOELBERG

This Christmas had begun like any other. The laughter of our happily excited children was evidence that Santa had indeed been able to decipher the hastily scrawled notes mailed weeks before.

As was our custom, LeRoy and I would wait until the children had sufficient time to inspect, test, compare, and segregate their new treasures before we would open our gifts.

The similarity of this Christmas to any other ended here.

The loud knock on the front door demanded immediate answer.

"Come quick!" There was urgency in our friend's voice. "I think you have a fire at your store!"

Fears flooded my mind as I ran through the vacant lot to the store, a small grocery business, which was not yet half paid for.

There were no flames rising from the building, but the windows were solid black.

A fireman came running up and put his hand against the window.

"No heat." He seemed relieved. "There's no fire now—let's open it up."

Our hopes were raised. Perhaps we had not lost everything!

He turned the key and pushed open the door. The dense, choking smoke that had filled every minute space of the small building drifted out into the street.

My heart sank. It was like looking at the inside of a coal-black furnace. Not a crack, not a corner, not one can stacked beneath another had escaped the ugly black filth!

LeRoy, with the help of some of the firemen, removed the motor that had burned itself out. We stood gazing in disbelief at the result.

True, the store had not burned, but was it salvageable? Perhaps the building and equipment could be cleaned, but what about the thousands of bottles, cans, and cartons? Even if they could be saved, how could we possibly survive the closing of business for even a few days?

"Only one thing to do." The fireman's voice was surprisingly cheerful. "Let's see if we can clean it up."

We were reluctant to accept his offer of help. After all, wasn't this Christmas, a day to be spent with family and loved ones?

"Come on," he joked. "My son will be glad to have me out of the house so that he can play with his electric train. Get me a bucket and some soap."

No sooner would we equip one volunteer with cleaning items than another would appear at the door, demanding, as one neighbor put it, "a chance to participate in this joyful holiday project."

Each person who came to the door uttered an astonished "Oh, no!" and then, "Where do you want me to start?"

By 11 A.M. there were over forty people: friends, neighbors, firemen, patrons, and new acquaintances, scrubbing away at the terrible black goo. Still they kept coming! We were overwhelmed!

The men had taken over the cleaning of the ceiling, the most stubborn and difficult task of all. The women were working in twos, taking items off the shelves, cleaning what they could, and boxing the rest.

One young lad who was recuperating from a broken leg

made trips to the cafe to get hamburgers and potato chips to feed the workers. Another brought turkey and rolls which, I'm certain, were to have been the biggest part of his family's Christmas dinner.

An energetic teenager must have run twenty miles emptying buckets and refilling them with clean hot water.

A service station operator brought hundreds of old cleaning rags.

An electrician worked on a motor replacement and soon had the refrigerator case operating again.

This was no ordinary cleaning job. Every inch had to be scrubbed, scoured, washed, and rinsed. Sometimes this procedure had to be repeated seven times before the white of the walls and ceiling would show through, yet everyone was laughing and joking as though they were having a good time.

"Actually, I only dropped by to supervise," came a comment from behind the bread rack.

"I bet this cures you of following fire trucks," a fireman chided his wife.

We all laughed when an attractive blonde woman, who was perched on top of the vegetable case and now bore a striking resemblance to a chimney sweep, burst out with a chorus of "Chim Chim Cheree."

It was shortly after 2 A.M. when we locked the front door. Everyone had gone. As they finished their jobs, they just slipped out—not waiting for a word of thanks or a smile of appreciation.

We walked home hand in hand. Tears flowed freely down my cheeks. Not the tears of frustration and despair that had threatened earlier, but tears of love and gratitude. Business would open as usual tomorrow—because fifty-four kind people had the true spirit of Christmas in their hearts.

Our children had left the tree lights burning, and our presents lay unopened in a neat pile on the floor. They would wait until morning. Whatever those gaily wrapped packages contained would be dwarfed, indeed, by the great gift of friendship given to us that Christmas Day.

Deseret News, December 21, 1970, p. 1. Reprinted by permission. LaRue Hale Soelberg and her husband, LeRoy Soelberg, Jr., are parents of eight children; they reside in Grantsville, Utah. Sister Soelberg is active in community affairs and teaches spiritual living in Relief Society.

H. Armstrong Roberts

Trouble at the Inn

DINA DONOHUE

For years now whenever Christmas pageants are talked about in a certain little town in the Midwest, someone is sure to mention the name of Wallace Purling. Wally's performance in one annual production of the nativity play has slipped into the realm of legend. But the old-timers who were in the audience that night never tire of recalling exactly what happened.

Wally was nine that year and in the second grade, though he should have been in the fourth. Most people in town knew that he had difficulty in keeping up. He was big and clumsy, slow in movement and mind. Still, Wally was well-liked by the other children in his class, all of whom were smaller than he, though the boys had trouble hiding their irritation when Wally would ask to play ball with them or any game, for that matter, in which winning was important.

Most often they'd find a way to keep him out, but Wally would hang around anyway—not sulking, just hoping. He was always a helpful boy, a willing and smiling one, and the natural protector, paradoxically, of the underdog. If the older boys chased the younger ones away, it would always be Wally who'd say, "Can't they stay? They're no bother."

Wally fancied the idea of being a shepherd with a flute in the Christmas pageant that year, but the play's director, Miss Lambard, assigned him to a more important role. After all, she reasoned, the innkeeper did not have too many lines, and Wally's size would make his refusal of lodging to Joseph more forceful.

So it happened that the usual large, partisan audience gathered for the town's yearly extravaganza of crooks and crèches, of beards, crowns, halos, and a whole stageful of squeaky voices. No one on stage or off was more caught up in the magic of the night than Wallace Purling. They said later that he stood in the wings and watched the performance with such fascination that from time to time Miss Lambard had to make sure he did not wander onstage before his cue.

Then came the time when Joseph appeared, slowly, tenderly guiding Mary to the door of the inn. Joseph knocked hard on the wooden door set into the painted backdrop. Wally the innkeeper was there, waiting.

"What do you want?" Wally said, swinging the door open with a brusque gesture.

"We seek lodging."

"Seek it elsewhere." Wally looked straight ahead but spoke vigorously. "The inn is filled."

"Sir, we have asked everywhere in vain. We have traveled far and are very weary."

"There is no room in this inn for you." Wally looked properly stern.

"Please, good innkeeper, this is my wife, Mary. She is heavy with child and needs a place to rest. Surely you must have some small corner for her. She is so tired."

Now for the first time, the innkeeper relaxed his stiff stance and looked down at Mary. With that, there was a long pause, long enough to make the audience a bit tense with embarrassment.

"No! Begone!" the prompter whispered from the wings.

"No!" Wally repeated automatically. "Begone!"

Joseph sadly placed his arm around Mary, and Mary laid her head upon her husband's shoulder, and the two of them started to move away. The innkeeper did not return inside the inn, however. Wally stood there in the doorway watching the forlorn couple. His mouth was open, his brow creased with concern, his eyes filling unmistakably with tears.

And suddenly this Christmas pageant became different from all others.

"Don't go, Joseph," Wally called out. "Bring Mary back." And Wallace Purling's face grew into a bright smile. "You can have *my* room."

Some people in town thought that the pageant had been ruined. Yet there were others—many, many others—who considered it the most Christmas of all Christmas pageants they had ever seen.

Reprinted by permission from *Guideposts Magazine,* copyright 1966 by Guideposts Associates, Inc., Carmel, New York 10512.

Again It Was Christmas Eve

DAVID O. McKAY

Christmas experiences in the Old Home were always joyous occasions. Perhaps the finest description of these days is contained in a letter written in 1938 by President McKay to his brother, Thomas E., who was at that time presiding in the Swiss-German Mission of The Church of Jesus Christ of Latter-day Saints.

Salt Lake City, Utah
December 12, 1938

My dear brother and playmate, Thomas E.,

I went to Huntsville the other day and visited the Old Home. It was a typical wintery day, so you can easily imagine how cold the rooms were in which no fires were burning, and in which none had been for weeks. The house was just like a large refrigerator.

There were a few things which I wanted to do so I threw your old coonskin coat over my shoulders and soon felt warm and comfortable. For a few moments I strolled leisurely from room to room, and, being in a reminiscent mood, I let my mind wander at will down the lanes of memory. I saw "Tommy" and "Dadie" go upstairs to bed, and felt the tender touch of the dearest, sweetest mother that ever lived as she tenderly tucked the bedclothes around her two roguish boys and gave them goodnight kisses.

Again it was Christmas Eve. Our stockings having been hung where Santa couldn't help but see them, we lay half expecting to hear the jingle of the sleigh bells announcing the approach of good old St. Nick to the chimney top—sleep came tardily, but finally the sandman succeeded in closing our eyes.

Christmas morning. I can see those boys creeping down the stairs before daybreak—no electric switch to press and flood the room with light; no flashlight at hand. They didn't even light the old kerosene lamp. Step by step they groped their way in the dark, and sought the nail (or chair) on which each had hung respectively his empty stocking. Who can ever forget the thrill of that first touch of the stocking filled with Santa's treasures! Apple in the toe, sticks of red and white candy protruding from the top, and trinkets and presents hidden in between! Perhaps a trumpet stuck out with the candies; but the drum and sled were standing nearby.

The air in the room was cold even though the last embers in the kitchen were still smouldering—evidence, if the boys had stopped to think, that father and mother had sat up late enough to welcome St. Nick to our house.

Soon the girls were awake also, and the lamp was lit—then the "oh's" and the "ah's," and the medley of sounds of drums, Jew's harp, harmonica, and music box!

As the sun came smiling over those snow-capped mountains, he turned the frost into diamonds that sparkled from the leafless trees and seemed to dance on the twelve-inch blanket of pure white snow.

Then came the playmates with their merry cry, "Christmas gift."

In the afternoon the children's dance! (One of those boys danced with a sweet little girl eleven successive times!) Oh, the romance of childhood!

Chores—evening shadows, supper and bed, and another Christmas was gone. Why, to childhood, is Christmas Day so short, and the next far away?

Christmas again, anticipated by the trip up South Fork to

get our own Christmas tree from the hillside. They were older then, those boys, but their stockings still were hung, and good old Santa never failed to fill them.

Summertime and the swimming hole in Spring Creek; baseball on the "square." Boys and girls strolling "across the creek," over on the knoll plucking flowers—daisies, bluebells, and the modest forget-me-nots, then leisurely back to town where we played croquet—parlor games in the evening where we had to redeem the forfeits!

Later came school and missions, yet still the tender ties that radiated from a devoted father and loving mother ever pulled us back to the Old Home, the dearest, sweetest spot on earth.

It is only an old country home, but no palace was ever filled with truer love and devotion on the part of parents, brothers, and sisters, than those which pervaded the hearts of the loved ones in that family circle.

Hanging your coat in its accustomed place, I walked out of the front door; as the night-latch clicked, I thought it might have been the click of the lid of a treasure chest that held the wealth of memories that no money could buy.

Well, my brother and pal of youthful days, I just wanted you to share with me this glimpse of happy memories, and to say, as the yuletide now approaches, my heart is full of loving wishes to you, that you and yours may enjoy the happiest Christmas ever, and that the New Year may come laden with happiness and joy supreme.

———————

Jeanette McKay Morrell, comp., *Highlights in the Life of President David O. McKay* (Salt Lake City: Deseret Book Co., 1966), pp. 29-31. David O. McKay, a brother of Sister Morrell, was the ninth president of The Church of Jesus Christ of Latter-day Saints. He was born September 8, 1873, at Huntsville, Utah, and died January 18, 1970.

The Wonderful Christmas Tree

REED BLAKE

et all the Saints . . . gather imme-
diately to the east bank of the [Missouri] river . . . or as soon as
they can, bringing their money, goods, and effects with them;
and, so far as they can consistently, gather young stock by the
way, which is much needed here and will be ready sale; and when
here, let all who can go directly over the mountains; and those
who cannot, let them go immediately to work at making im-
provements, raising grain and stock on the lands recently vacated
by the Potawatomi Indians and owned by the United States,
and by industry . . . their young cattle will grow into teams; by
interchange of labor they can raise their own grain and provision,
and build their own wagons; . . . thus speedily and comfortably
procure an outfit. . . ." (General Epistle from the Council of the
Twelve Apostles, December 23, 1847.)

Red ribbons indicated the ends of the two braids that struck
her midway down her back. They were blonde, with overtones of
brown. Her eyes, as she watched the man who had just come up
the road, were typically those of one who is eleven—now intent,
now curious, now openly happy. Her name was Nan, she said,
"and this is Fredrick. He's fourteen."

"And doing a man's work, I can tell that," the man
answered.

"Are you from around here?" the boy asked, standing a little taller in his too-short pants, his black hair jutting over his ears.

"No," the man said. "I have come from Iowa Territory."

"My father is in Iowa," the girl spoke quickly.

The man smiled.

In the sod house Elizabeth Harmony Small Duncan put the water on to boil and went out to the cellar to fetch some potatoes. It was an open winter, as those still living on the Potawatomi lands called it; it was now the 23rd of December and there had been only one flurry of snow—it had melted in an hour—in late November. Harvard wrote that it was heaven-sent, enabling him to stay longer in Iowa, working for landowners there and taking his pay in corn and grain and sometimes even in gold coin.

This, of course, was the history of the gathering—not just for them, but for hundreds of others. They had started from Arkansas the summer before, traveling up the river by steamboat and out-fitting themselves at Keokuk (when they used up the last of their money), then going west across the Iowa Territory and across the Missouri River. Here in an abandoned sod hut Harvard had left the family while he returned to work as long as the weather would hold.

But Christmas! Couldn't he come home for Christmas and then go back, if there were work still to go back to? Surely Zion could wait for Christmas. But in her heart Elizabeth knew that it couldn't. There was precious little here: a good wagon made from sturdy wood from the Mississippi bottom, but nothing in it. He should work as long as he could.

In the distance she could see the rolling hills—hills that were as wrinkles in a quilt compared to the mountains they had yet to cross and canyons to traverse. That was the barrier that stopped east from going west, the barrier that had stopped them for nine months already. During the day the shading of the hills had been shifting. Above the hills, clouds gathered and dispersed and gathered again, the green on the cedar-dotted bluffs varying from black to green. Now a dark bank of clouds came rolling in, obscuring the gray of the broad valley of the Platte, covering the full flush of the late afternoon sun and bringing with it,

Elizabeth knew, a snowfall that would soon be measured in inches.

As Elizabeth rounded the house with the potatoes, she was startled to see the stranger. She clutched the load tightly and hoped the man wouldn't see the fear in her eyes.

Elizabeth's fears, however, soon proved groundless. The young stranger introduced himself as Stefan Groff, a Mormon who, like themselves, was going west. His parents and sisters had remained in New York. He was planning to cross the mountains now so that, when spring came, he could plant seeds and build a cabin. Then his family would follow him west next summer. Meanwhile, he said, his father was working in a print shop in New York.

"When we arrived in America, we were out of money," he added.

"Are you from Europe?" Elizabeth asked. He nodded and smiled. "In our town in Bavaria, we could speak the best English of anyone, my family and I; but over here we find it not so good."

"It isn't the words," Elizabeth assured him. "It's the way they sound. But your English is really very good."

"I think it's not so bad," he said. She looked toward the west. "Can you cross the mountains in the snow?"

"I am a good walker in the snow," he said. "I will walk to Fort Kearney. There I will buy a mount and cross in company with the first riders to make the trip."

He offered to help the children do their evening chores, to chop wood, to milk the cow, to do whatever else he could in exchange for a night's lodging. He had hoped to reach the Henderson cabin, which by his calculation should be another seven miles, but with a storm approaching and darkness upon him he didn't think it wise to continue his journey.

"We would be pleased to have you," Elizabeth said. "Have you traveled far today?"

"About thirty-seven miles," he answered.

When she seemed surprised at the distance, he added, "I always walk close to forty miles. It's just a good day's walk."

Suddenly a flicker of hope came into her voice. "How do

you know the Hendersons?" she asked. "Have you been working
with Carl Henderson in Iowa?"

"No," he answered. "I have been walking these past weeks
—all the distance from New York. I met the man Henderson on
the trail near the Elkhorn. He offered me his place to rest. He's
bringing a wagonload of goods, he and another man. The wagon is
old, the load heavy."

"Stefan," she said, the excitement coming to her voice, "you
could be a 'Santeklas.' Tell me, did the other man have black hair
and a brown overcoat?"

"The other man was called Harv."

"Oh, Stefan," she cried, "how many days behind you is he?"

Elizabeth waited until supper to tell the children. Now the
emotion of the moment overcame her as she said, " 'Santeklas'
has something to say."

Stefan looked startled, then said, "Sleeping down the road
this night is a man called Harv Duncan. And he will be home
for Christmas."

To call him "Santeklas" delighted the children, and when
Elizabeth told them to stop, Stefan said to let them continue;
he didn't mind. They sat around the fire and talked about Iowa
and how their father had looked when Stefan saw him, what he
was doing, and what he had said. When the talk drifted to Stefan,
he told them that he and his family were all converts to the
Church and had been baptized two years ago. He traced his family's voyage across Europe and the Atlantic Ocean and his own
journey across the United States to the frontier. Nan was cap-
tivated by the young man, who brought still more joy or excitement or happiness with each new breath. When he was
finished, she said, "Stefan, tell us about Christmas."

"All right," Stefan said. "I will tell you a story from the
old country—a story from Bavaria."

"From Bavaria?" the children echoed.

"Yes, from Bavaria," he said, speaking faster now, warming
to the subject. "From the beautiful forests of the Bavarian Alps.
There on a Christmas Eve long ago, a tiny knock came to the
door of a small but warm cottage standing all alone in a forested
vale."

"All alone like we're all alone?" asked Nan.

The man nodded. "In this home lived a forester and his family, and when they opened the door to the tiny knock, there stood a small child in the snow, cold and hungry and very tired. The family took the child in and warmed him by their fire. And while their lot was a very simple one, they nevertheless gave him their best clothes, fed him their best food, and bade him sleep in their best bed.

"In the morning the family awoke to see the child standing over them, glowing as they had never before seen a person glow. The child said, 'I can give you nothing beyond what you already have, except one thing.' The child went from the house and broke a branch from a fir tree nearby and planted it by the door. Instantly it blossomed.

" 'Here is my gift to you,' he said. 'Henceforth it shall always bear fruit at Christmastide, when all the rest of the world is empty and dead.' The child smiled and left, saying, 'To you it shall be a sign of faith that does not die.' "

The room was silent. The fire was dying, and outside the wind came up stronger, pushing against the door. Nan spoke first. "I wish we could have that kind of Christmas."

Young Fredrick added, "We've got the cottage and the love. That's what the story was about—the love the Savior brought."

Stefan stood with his back to the fire. "Well," he said, "since you've got everything else in the legend, and since I'm the visitor and it's nearly Christmas Eve, perhaps I should produce a tree."

"Can you?" gasped Nan.

"I can," Stefan said. "I will."

The next day passed slowly for Nan and Fredrick, and even for Elizabeth, as the clouds began to shed large, silent flakes. Then when the darkness made it seem as if evening had come, but in reality it was only four o'clock, Fredrick, who had stationed himself at the west window most of the day, let out a yelp and ran from the cabin. Nan dropped her embroidery work and followed.

Striding down the road, his forearm bent across the stump of a tree, came Stefan. "You've been to the hills," Elizabeth said, and he replied, as she knew he would, that it was only a good day's walk.

"It isn't a fir," he said to the children. "It's a cedar, but an evergreen nonetheless."

"It's the beautiful Christmas tree—just like the story," said Nan.

They placed the tree in a bucket and packed it with stones to hold it erect. Then Elizabeth brought out a white tablecloth and placed it around the bottom. The tree looked as if it were on the hillside again, growing skyward out of the snow.

"What shall we do for blossoms?" asked Nan.

"We could start with those pretty ribbons in your hair," Stefan answered.

"Really?" Nan squealed. Before anyone could answer her, she had them off and on the tree.

They spent an hour decorating the tree. Fredrick took string from his pocket and strung it through a pretty picture cut into squares from *Godey's Lady's Book*. Elizabeth found a sugar sack stuffed with odds and ends of clothing that would someday become a rag rug. They tied some of them into bows, rolled them into balls, and tied them at the top; they tore others into long strips and draped them from branch to branch.

Even Stefan made a contribution to the tree. He tied six five-inch willows together at the center to make a star, covered it with his red and black handkerchief, and secured it to the top of the tree.

"It's a wonderful star!" Nan exclaimed.

When the tree was all decorated, Stefan bade his farewell. The children were still calling "We'll see you in Zion" long after the tall man was lost from view, the words falling on the whiteness of the earth.

Then the door was closed on the approaching night, the curtains were pulled back from the two windows, and a lamp was placed in each.

Improvement Era, December 1968, pp. 6-9. Reed Blake, a former member of the *Era* staff, teaches sociology and social psychology at Brigham Young University. The father of three children, he is a doctoral candidate at Utah State University. This story stems from early family records.

A Beautiful Silver Star

IVAN T. ANDERSON

When the Allied forces made their big push into Germany it was the duty of my military police battalion to take prisoners from the front lines into crudely constructed stockades.

I shall never forget December 24, 1944, and the German prisoner of war who helped to make it memorable for me.

It was a bitter cold night and I found myself on duty helping to guard more than twelve hundred German prisoners.

To say we were a homesick group of men would be an understatement. The fact that it was Christmas Eve only added to our depression.

One of our company, a man from the Smoky Mountains of Tennessee, stopped blowing on his hands long enough to say:

"What a cold, miserable Christmas! Just because we are stuck out here doesn't mean we can't do something about it. I'm going out and find a tree."

"Forget it!" another M.P. shouted. "There are no trees around here; besides, we haven't anything to decorate with anyway."

Not to be discouraged, Smoky went into the darkness and later returned with a bedraggled specimen.

"You call that thing a tree?" our heckler continued. "In Texas we'd plow that under for a bush."

With a positive attitude, Smoky began to decorate his tree with ornaments made from gum wrappers, candy wrappers, etc.

Several of the men not stationed directly at the stockade began to help our zealous friend with his seemingly impossible task.

As we worked I suddenly heard a voice calling from the stockade: "American, American."

Turning toward the compound I saw a German prisoner with one hand extended through the barbed wire. With his other hand he was motioning toward me.

I quickly threw a shell into the chamber of my rifle and approached him with caution. What I saw in his hand astounded me.

This prisoner had made a beautiful silver star, entirely from gum foil, that was a work of art. He placed the star in my hand and motioned to the top of our tree.

Hoping he spoke some English, I said: "This star has such detail, are you a professional artist?"

By his puzzled expression it was obvious he spoke no more English than I spoke German, so I took his contribution over and placed it atop our tree.

"Well, I'll be!" heckler began again. "I hate to admit this, but that bush is beginning to look like a real tree. Guess I should have kept my mouth shut, eh, Smoky?" (A loud cheer of agreement resounded from all the men.)

As we completed our tree we began singing Christmas carols, and I noticed several of the prisoners joined in on "Silent Night."

The last strains were fading into the night when I heard the same voice call: "American."

This time the prisoner had both hands extended through the barbed wire.

Again I approached with caution, rifle ready, and again I was amazed at what he held in his hands.

This German sculptor had made intricate figures of Joseph, Mary, and the Christ Child. He pointed under our tree as he handed me his detailed work.

I nodded my thanks and carefully placed the delicate figures where he had indicated.

As I placed the tiny figure of the Christ Child, made from a stick base and professionally covered with foil, the light from our fire actually seemed to give it a heavenly glow. I thought of how far we had strayed from the teachings of Jesus and felt tears sting my eyes.

Looking at the stockade, I saw the prisoner was still behind the barbed wire, so I hurried back, smiled, and warmly shook his hand.

He returned my smile and the firelight caught the tears that were in his eyes.

Since the close of World War II I have thought of this German prisoner of war numerous times.

Our meeting was brief; we were two ships that passed in the night, and yet I feel this man would agree that our only hope for a lasting world peace would be a return to the teachings of the tiny figure he so beautifully molded that cold December night. One thing is certain: if we love the Lord we also have a genuine concern for all mankind—the two are synonymous.

Deseret News, December 24, 1970, p. 1. Reprinted by permission. Ivan T. Anderson, an employee at Hill Air Force Base in Utah, has often wondered what happened to this German prisoner of war. The story was written by his wife, Jettie Jacob Anderson, a teacher of English and speech. They have two children.

She Was Baptized on Christmas Eve

STEVEN RAY AFFLECK

My companion and I started what we called the "new move-in" program, where we called on people who had recently moved in, to welcome them into the area and see if we could teach them something about the Church. Working through this program, we met a lady from England and her family. At this time her husband was in Vietnam. She was very interested in learning about the Church, strictly from an educational standpoint. We talked to her for about five weeks, and after that period of time she had a strong desire to bring her family of four into the Church. However, for this she needed her husband's permission.

One day shortly before Christmas she said to me: "Elder Affleck, the greatest Christmas present I could have would be to be baptized into the Church and receive the Holy Ghost, and see my family baptized." On that day, December 22, she wrote a letter to Vietnam, telling her husband about the Church and asking for permission to be baptized.

At one o'clock the next morning we got a phone call from this woman. She couldn't wait to tell us the news. That same afternoon she had received a letter from her husband in which he said: "Leslie, I have found the most wonderful thing! It means more to me in this life than anything. A young man who is in my platoon is a Mormon, and he took me to a meeting here in Saigon. I have joined the Mormon Church." Then he went into specific details about how she çould contact the elders.

What a wonderful blessing this family had received! She was baptized on Christmas Eve.

As I read my journal now, I remember how homesick I was that Christmas, but I also remember how very thankful I was for the baptisms we had and for the Spirit of the Lord, which governed us.

Instructor, June 1969, pp. 200-201. Steven Ray Affleck wrote this story while he was attending Brigham Young University, based on an experience in the Great Lakes Mission. He and his wife, the former Karin Lochhead, reside in Denver and have three children.

Who Ever Heard of a Crippled Angel?

JANICE BECKSTEAD

The stage was very quiet now, so unlike the hustle and bustle of the past few weeks. I sat there alone in the place they had finally decided would be the least awkward for them and for me.

The words "If she's going to be in it at all, she'll have to be on stage and in her place before anyone else gets here!" still rang in my ears.

I had really tried at rehearsals to be as inconspicuous as possible, but no matter how many attempts we made, my crutches just didn't add to the angel's entrance. You see, that's what I was supposed to be—an angel. And "Who ever heard of a crippled angel?" My good leg kicked my crutches farther under the riser.

Tears welled in my eyes as I thought how ridiculous I was going to look when the curtain opened—the only angel, sitting on the front row with left leg thrust straight out front, encased in a bandage from thigh to ankle. "Everyone knows the angels appeared after Christ's birth and not before."

If they had only let me play the part of Mary I could have sat with my leg hidden behind the manger, but apparently no one could picture Mary as an eleven-year-old blonde with freckles, so the part of Mary went to one of the older and prettier girls, who had long dark hair. Again I kicked the crutches, but this time for the freckles.

"Before anyone else gets here. . . !" meant just that. So I had managed the back stairs, heavy curtains, and dimly lit stage by myself. I glanced up at the star, now dark, and muttered, "Well, you're one thing that has given them as much trouble as me. You haven't lit up at the right time yet!" Tears welled again.

I had always felt that the annual Christmas cantata presented by the school really set the proper mood for the holiday season. The weeks of rehearsals, relearning the carols, scenery, costumes, makeup, all retelling the story that grows more beautiful with each telling.

I remembered how anxious I was after surgery to get out of the hospital, on crutches, and back to school in time for the final rehearsals.

I loved to sing and supposed that was why they were putting up with me at all.

Each year the theme was the same, but the presentation varied. This year as the curtain opened, Joseph, Mary, and the baby Jesus would be on stage surrounded by the shepherds and wise men. The star would illuminate the sky (if they could get it to work). Angels would be heard singing softly offstage. As the shepherds and wise men knelt and presented their gifts to the Christ Child the backdrops would open and the angels in their white robes, singing "Silent Night," would enter and take their places on the risers.

Noticing the shaking of heads and worried glances among teachers as I tried to make this planned entrance, I would sing out with all I had, hoping to make up for the inconvenience I was causing. I guess my enthusiasm made me unaware of the debate among the "powers that be" as to whether or not I should even be in the play. Unaware, that is, until this very afternoon of the performance. "If she's going to be in it at all, she'll have to be on stage before. . . !" They had reached a compromise.

The dim blue lights gave the stage an almost unreal effect. I shifted my position. Already my leg was starting to ache.

Suddenly I wanted this night and especially the performance

to be over. I didn't feel enthusiastic any more and didn't see how I could sing with a lump in my throat so big it made me constantly blink back the tears.

Then, as if in answer to my thoughts, the curtains on the far side opened and in stepped Joseph and Mary. Very carefully Mary laid a tiny bundle in the manger.

Without a word, the tall stately Joseph took his place beside her, resting his hand protectively on her shoulder. They neither spoke nor glanced my way, content to keep watch over the manger. As to what happened next, I can only guess—the right combination of switches, an elusive connection, or the spirit of the occasion, but the star came on and it stayed on!

One by one shepherds appeared, carrying crude wooden chests or grains from the field. I blinked hard. Were these the same boys that had pushed, shoved, and tripped with their crooks all during practice? Here they were transformed into humble shepherds. Look! the three wise men—what handsome long robes and jeweled turbans. In their hands, oh, yes, I know—gold, frankincense, and myrrh. They too were humbled by what they saw.

As the curtain slowly opened, all eyes were on the tiny figure in the manger. It was so quiet I hardly dared breathe. Somewhere far away I could hear singing—"Silent night, holy night." It came nearer and nearer. Suddenly the sky parted and all around us angels were singing, "Christ the Savior is born."

Once again the eyes of the world turned to this, the most beautiful of all scenes. But for me it was suddenly more than just a scene. It was as though I had actually been there that first Christmas night. Now the tears spilled freely and with all the voice I could squeeze past the swelling in my heart, I too whispered, "Christ the Savior is born!"

Deseret News, December 23, 1970. p. 1. Reprinted by permission. Janice Andrus Beckstead, a native of Draper, Utah, has three children. The family lives in Crescent, Utah.

God Has Said Merry Christmas to Me

ANNA W. McNEIL

Grandma Westlin had often heard and used the expression "a square peg in a round hole," or "a round peg in a square hole," little dreaming that these descriptions would ever apply to herself. Then, one day, things happened with terrible suddenness, and her well-ordered little world dissolved into chaos. Grandma, sitting dazed and numb, did not know how to cope with the new state of affairs. Grandpa had seemed so strong and well in spite of his years that the thought of an all-alone future had never occurred to her.

"Grandma had better make her home with us," suggested prosperous John Westlin to his wife.

So the arrangements were made before Grandma realized what they were all about, and the next few days found her transplanted from the peaceful Southern village where she had spent her seventy-five useful years to a strictly modern city apartment. Grandma had often grieved over a tree that had been uprooted by a storm, its boughs still clinging tenaciously to a thread of life and its leaves bravely putting forth their green. How like her own experience, she reflected; but then, she mustn't be gloomy. How good John and his wife were to provide a home for her, and how appreciative she must be. There was so much she could still do for them—her sight was good and her fingers nimble.

"This is your room, Grandma," announced Mrs. Westlin, ushering her into a beautifully appointed chamber. "Now, you are not expected to do a thing, you know, only to make yourself comfortable and be as happy as you can, under the circumstances."

Grandma looked about a little fearfully. It wasn't the cheery coziness she had been accustomed to, and from the sixth-floor window the street below yawned like a chasm. But she faced her tall granddaughter-in-law with a gallant spirit.

"It's good of you, Winifred, to do all this for me, and you mustn't spoil me by letting me set around. I want to earn my board and keep," she ventured.

"Oh, no, Grandma! If you care for your own room that is quite all you can do."

Nevertheless, the first meal over, Grandma produced a crisp gingham apron and stepped gingerly over the waxed floors toward the kitchen.

"I'm all ready to do the dishes, dearie," she said, brightly. "Now, just tell me where you keep the dishpan and the wipers and then I'll always know." She peered about in vain.

"We have no dishpan. We have an electrical dishwasher." Mrs. Westlin indicated the device. "You might just as well take your apron off, Grandma, for there's absolutely nothing you can do."

No one was in the habit of disputing that particular tone in Mrs. Westlin's voice, but Grandma was intent upon being useful. "There's the darning!" she exclaimed. "Now you find me all your stockings and all of John's socks, and let me look them over. I'll mend them so you will surely think they are brand new."

"We never wear mended hose. Come, Grandma," she suggested, "you want to take a nap, don't you? Here's a flower for you to take up to your room." She chose a huge, feathery chrysanthemum from a cluster in a tall vase.

Grandma accepted it thankfully. She was too tactful to say that she never took a nap in the daytime. She untied her apron, folded it carefully, and laid it away.

After that, Grandma did not offer to assist with the housework. She appeared at meals her bright, pleasant self—and then went to her lonely room where she invented a diversion that consisted of thinking what would be going on every hour of the day if she were back in her old home. She knew which of the neighbors would be running in at different times, who would want to borrow, who would ask for a recipe, who was working for some of the church interests and needed her help, who had a ticket to sell, who would call out, "Want anything at the store today, Grandma?", who would stop with the mail, and how the children homeward bound from school would congregate about the porch while she generously handed out freshly made cookies and doughnuts. At last, even this palled, because Grandma became frankly homesick. Yet, what to do she didn't know. A family had taken possession of the house. She could not reconcile herself to boarding elsewhere in the village, because the thought of home meant doing the things she liked.

"I know what!" Inspiration came to her. "I'll sew!" But sew what? Then she was seized with a happy idea. Back in the village days, Grandma had clothed dozens of dolls, not only for her little friends, but for the various barrels which from time to time were packed by the church workers for missionary centers at home and abroad. She had a bag of pieces which represented many odds and ends of dress materials and trimmings, and this she had brought with her.

"The women all seem to be so busy in this city," mused Grandma, judging by what she had seen and heard in the Westlin household, "that I don't believe they think of such a thing as making doll dresses for their children. The flimsy clothes that the store-bought dolls wear can't last, the way children handle them; and when I was a little girl, I wanted my dolls to have plenty of changes." She indulged in a rare smile, thinking of the contrast between the now and then, in dolls and their costumes, as in everything else.

One idea suggested another, and Grandma, for want of something to pass the time, had become an inveterate newspaper reader. For the first time in her life, she composed an advertisement. Her fingers held the pencil stiffly, and she made many erasures before it was written to her satisfaction, but she was pleased with the result.

"Mrs. Santa Claus would like to make clothes for dolls. Busy mothers, please notice." Then followed her name, naively set down as *Grandma Westlin,* and her address. She especially liked the thought of "Mrs." Santa Claus.

Keyed to the highest pitch with anticipation, she emptied the bag of pieces on her bed, sorted them out, and even threaded several needles to save time when the real operations should begin. . . . Hour by hour the shining needles flew in and out, and little garments took form like magic.

One of the delighted mothers slipped a five-dollar bill in Grandma's hand. "I insist on your taking it," she said. "I can't sew to save my life, and my little girl has been simply crazy for a new outfit for her favorite doll."

Five dollars! Grandma blinked at the bill and touched it unbelievingly.

Interrupting her unaccustomed line of financial thought, the doorbell rang insistently, and the maid, displeased, ushered a small boy into Grandma's presence. He was clean but threadbare, and his hands were blue with cold.

"Are you the lady what calls herself Missus Santy Claus?" he asked. "I read yer ad and I brought yer this doll to fix up for my kid sister. She's lame."

He deposited a bundle in Grandma's lap. She unrolled layers of newspaper and discovered a doll—an evident aristocrat among dolls in spite of the fact that one arm and one leg were missing and that she was sadly rumpled. Little frozen clumps of ashes clung to her, and smears of coal disfigured her face. But she had curly bobbed hair and flirty blue eyes with long lashes, and her initial cost had probably been large.

Grandma surveyed doll and boy with interest. "Where did you get this?" she inquired.

"Out'n the ashcan over there." He indicated the direction with a jerk of his thumb. "I hunt in the ashcans ev'ry night. Sometimes I find things to take home to my sister. She can't walk, and she's always askin' for a doll. But this didn't have no clothes on, so I brought it to you to git dressed."

"How did you know about me?" pursued Grandma, kindly.

"My mother is advertisin' for work and I was lookin' over

the want ads to see if hers was in. That's how I come across yours."

"Have you a father?"

"My father is dead, and my mother goes out washin' and cleanin'."

"Has your little sister always been lame?"

"No'm. She was just like any other little girl till that sickness went around three or four years ago that left so many kids lame. But she don't seem to mind, Jennie don't. She makes up stories for herself, just as if she was readin', and she sings to herself for comp'ny. She's nine years old," he volunteered. "The neighbors like her, and sometimes they come and set with her while Ma and me are workin'. I sell newspapers. I'm only twelve, and you have to be a lot older to get a real job. If I could earn enough money, my mother would never have to go out to work. I'd see to that."

"I know you would," said Grandma, with approval. She knew exactly what she would do in a case like this if she were in her own home with her own kitchen at her disposal. But in the home of another! "Day after tomorrow's Christmas," she meditated aloud. "I'll have to work quick. Well, sonny, you be sure and come back tomorrow night, and the doll will be all ready for your little sister."

"How much will the clothes cost?" he asked. He counted out a few hoarded pennies. "Will it be more than that? Maybe you won't think this is enough."

"It's enough," said Grandma. His face shone so that her heart glowed responsively.

Surely no doll was ever dressed with more loving care. The choicest remnant in the bag of pieces was a bit of pink calico, and Grandma cut into it happily. Little lengths of white muslin and edging were transformed into apparel of which any doll might well be proud, and the pink calico made such a gay little dress that it would bring cheer into the grayest surroundings.

Grandma next turned her attention to making an arm and a leg. Tightly rolled cotton and cloth answered the purpose, and Grandma attached them to the doll's body with pride. She brushed the tangled hair strand by strand and restored the soiled

face to its original cleanliness. Her efforts were repaid by a doll
so irresistible that she cuddled it as if she were seven years old
instead of seventy-five. Eagerly, she told the story to her grandson, enjoying his interest at sight of the rejuvenated doll. "And
that, John," she said, indicating the pink calico, "is a piece of the
dress your own father wore when he was two years old and having his first picture taken. It lay in a chest in the attic for years
—seemed as if I was too fond of it to ever use it. Then, thought
I, what's the use of keeping it, and I tucked it right into my bag
of pieces. And how glad I am that I did. I can hardly wait for
that boy to come back."

Next morning Grandma scanned the advertising columns
of the *Daily News* as was her custom ever since her own profit-
able advertisement had appeared. Something stood out on the
closely printed page in letters that seemed to her an inch high.

"Little girl is grieving for favorite doll, thrown into ashcan
by mistake. Five dollars reward if returned."

"This very doll!" gasped Grandma. And here it was all
ready for a little crippled girl who had never owned a doll and
was praying that Santa Claus would bring her one.

"With my five dollars and the five dollars reward," reasoned
Grandma, "why, we'll have some kind of a Christmas for her
after all. But land alive! I'll have to get a doll with a store-bought
dress. And mercy me, how will I ever get around in the stores
in the Christmas rush?"

The house was deserted. John did not come home at noon;
the maid had received permission to do a personal errand, and
Mrs. Westlin was investigating cases that had come to the attention of the charity committee of her club. Grandma felt that she
ought not to delay, and that since it was not far to the address
of the grieving little girl, she should make the trip alone.

She ascended the brown stone steps of an imposing resi-
dence and rang the entrance bell. The door opened, and she
entered a great room with an open fireplace. A child's delighted cry rang out, and a little girl with curls like burnished
gold hurled herself into Grandma's arms and took her and the
doll together in an embrace that almost took Grandma's breath
away.

Then there was the story to tell to an interested group who wanted to learn all about Mrs. Santa Claus, the bag of pieces, the newsboy who found the doll in an ashcan, and the little crippled girl. In the center of the group stood the happy little mother, with her restored treasure, hugging her doll and waiting her turn to tell how the new nursemaid, thinking it was of no value because it was minus an arm and a leg, and likewise clothing (its dress was being laundered for Christmas), had tossed the cherished doll into the ashes and how bad she felt when she learned that it was the one loved above all others. When she hurried to find it, it was gone.

There is no eloquence like that which comes from the heart, and Grandma did not seem like a plain old lady in black, telling a story that had largely to do with a piece of pink calico that had once been her baby boy's dress. It was as if the spirit of Christmas itself was speaking, and every hearer warmed to the appeal.

The little girl and her mother and father bundled Grandma into a big, luxurious automobile and insisted on taking her on a shopping trip that knew no limitations. If Grandma became tired she did not realize it in the least, for the simple reason that she was too happy to sense fatigue.

They did not stop at buying one doll—or two—or three; they added warm bedding, clothing, a Christmas tree with shining ornaments, books, toys, and even a plant with red flowers. Grandma was finally persuaded into going to her room to rest, with the assurance that the others would call for her in the evening to deliver the gifts in person. The wealthy father of the little girl took all the more interest because he was on the friendliest of terms with John Westlin.

At the time appointed, the small newsboy came, quivering with hope. "Is the doll all dressed?" he asked, peering about, vainly looking for it.

"Not the doll you found but another just as nice," said Grandma, and she opened the dresser drawer and heaped his arms with dolls large and small.

"Gee!" he exclaimed, . . . and then words failed, and he could only stare first at the precious armful and then at Grandma until his eyes blurred over with tears of joy.

"Well, you know I'm Mrs. Santa Claus," said Grandma briskly, getting into her hat and coat, for the automobile was at the door. "Now come and show me where you live, and we will give your little sister a Christmas that is a Christmas! And me one, too," she added under her breath. Grandma had learned long years before that Christmas has very little to do with the giving of gifts but very much with the giving of self.

The neighbors stared when the handsome car rolled into their narrow street. The gifts were carried upstairs by many willing hands and placed outside the door until it was discovered that the crippled girl was soundly asleep. An empty stocking had been pinned where Santa Claus could not fail to see it, for she was sure that he would find the way to her sometime, even if he never had before.

There was nothing in the room outside of bare necessities. "But it's clean—oh, scrupulously clean!" thought Grandma, looking about with the satisfaction of an expert housekeeper, as she went on tiptoe, placing the gifts.

The tree was set up and quickly, deftly trimmed. It sparkled as if it understood. A warm, comfortable blanket was thrown over the bed, and pretty new clothing arranged where the little girl's unbelieving eyes would see it the first thing on Christmas morning.

As they left, after a long, satisfied look, the little rich girl tugged at Grandma's arm. "You believe in Santa Claus, don't you?" she asked, blue eyes wide in her own happy faith.

"Bless your heart, I always have believed in him, and I always will," assured Grandma, folding her close.

"Then what do you want Santa to bring you for Christmas the very most of all?"

"If I whisper, you must never tell a soul in this world," cautioned Grandma, "for even Santa Claus can't give me my heart's desire. But when you see him, just say to him for me that the thing that Grandma wants most is to have her old home back again."

"Where is your old home, Grandma?" Somehow the little girl felt like crying without knowing why.

"It's back in the country, dear, many and many a mile from

here, a little white house with green blinds. In summer, there's the loveliest garden!" Grandma, taking her by the hand, added detail after detail, because it was so seldom these days that anyone seemed interested in her affairs.

For hours the little girl pondered the tale that Grandma told. She had given her promise not to tell "a soul in this world," but she was not quite sure if Santa Claus answered that description or not. She finally appealed to her father.

"Daddy, is Santa Claus 'a soul in this world'?" she inquired. "Because if he is not, I must write a letter to him."

"No, you couldn't exactly call him 'a soul in this world', for Santa Claus is surely not like the rest of us. When you speak of a 'soul in this world' you mean people," he answered, understandingly. "So now write your letter."

Patiently the little girl toiled, unwilling to ask for help in composition or spelling for fear that she would have to divulge Grandma's confidence. So it came about that on Christmas Day her father called on John Westlin to explain the circumstances and put a letter addressed to Santa Claus in his hands.

"Dear Santa Claus," he read. "This is for Grandma. She is not truly my grandmother but she is everybody's grandmother. She said I must not tell a soul in this world only you, but Daddy says you are not a soul in this world, but she wants you to give her back her old home. It is a white house ever so far back in the country, and she cried when she told me about it. She was very happy there. I don't think she is happy now, but she did not say so, so please, dear Santa Claus, give it back to her, please, please do."

"What am I to do?" said John Westlin, deeply affected. "I didn't realize that Grandma was miserable. After all, it's cruelty, in spite of our best intentions, to uproot old people from their homes. I only thought that Grandma ought not to be living by herself at her age. I might have known that she would be better off where she knows everybody and could do as she pleased."

"This is only a suggestion," offered his friend, "and you may not want to consider it, but let me tell you the story of last night. It would be an ideal place for those two children and their widowed mother, and the woman could look out for Grandma

and spare her the heavy part of the work. We can investigate
the case and make sure it is worthy. Personally, I cannot doubt
that it is."

On Christmas night, dinner was served in the Westlin home
with ceremony. Grandma, dressed in her best black silk with
white fichu and cameo pin, dutifully ate in silence, because she
was present only in body, her spirit being back in the old home,
living over again the rollicking Christmas days of other years.
There had been a formal exchange of gifts.

Grandma got back to her room a bit stumblingly. She
wouldn't dictate to Providence, but perhaps the good Lord
might mercifully let her spend her Christmas with Grandpa.

"I guess I'll get me to bed now," she thought. "God's in
his heaven; it's all right."

On the pillow lay an envelope with a gay Christmas seal.
It was addressed to her, and she opened it wonderingly, looking
for the signature first of all. When she read "Santa Claus" she
gave a tremulous little laugh.

Her hands shook so that she had difficulty in reading the
strong, masculine handwriting that said:

Grandma: Your wish has been made known to me. Your little white
home with green blinds away back in the country is waiting for you to come
back to it. I can't take you there in my sleigh drawn by my reindeer, much
as I would like to; but my messenger has bought a railroad ticket that will
take you there just as soon as you are ready to start.
Your friend,
Santa Claus

Grandma read the letter over and over again before she
fully comprehended its meaning. Then she gave a quavering
little scream that John Westlin, waiting outside her door, heard
with a gulp in his throat. He hurried into the room, and Grandma threw herself into his arms, laughing and crying all in one
breath. "What do you think?" she exclaimed, her old happy self
again. "God has said 'Merry Christmas' to me!"

In the meantime, a second letter was in the hands of the
little girl, and it too was signed "Santa Claus." "Oh, Daddy,"
she cried, "what does this part of it mean?" And he, with a
volume of Eugene Field's poems on his knees, turned the pages
and found the lines:

You are too young to know it now,
But sometime you will know.

This was the message:

Dear Little Girl:

Did you know that Christmas is not just one day in the year? It is every day, because the real Christmas is in your heart. Whenever you do anything for anybody because you love him, you have heard the echo of the angels' song of peace and goodwill. . . . May the beautiful Christmas spirit abide with you always.

And to make you very happy indeed, Santa Claus has bought Grandma's old home, and she is going back to stay there as long as she lives. The little lame girl and her mother and brother will make their home with Grandma, too, and by another Christmas the little lame girl will be strong and well.

I am glad that you wrote me that letter. It will be our secret and we will not tell "a soul in the world."

Your friend, now and always,

Santa Claus

Improvement Era, December 1934, pp. 718-20ff. Note: This story is fiction.

When the Wise Man Appeared

WILLIAM ASHLEY ANDERSON

It was a bitterly cold night, vast and empty. Over Hallett's Hill a brilliant star danced like tinsel on the tip of a Christmas tree. The still air was as resonant as the inside of an iron bell; but within our snug farmhouse in the Pocono Mountains of Pennsylvania it was mellow with the warmth of our cherry-red stoves.

The dinner things had been cleared away, and I relaxed when Bruce came downstairs—an apparition in a long white nightgown with a purple cloak of tintexed cotton over his shoulders. In one hand he held a tall crown of yellow pasteboard and tinsel. From the other swung an ornate censer. On his feet were thin flapping sandals.

"What in the world are you supposed to be?" I asked.

My wife looked at the boy critically, but with concern and tenderness.

"He's one of the Wise Men of the East!" she explained with some indignation.

The look she gave me was an urgent reminder that I had promised to get him to the schoolhouse in town in time for the Christmas pageant. I shuddered at the thought of the cold and went out into the night, pulling on a heavy coat.

The battery in the old car had gone dead, but by one of those freaks of mechanical whimsy, the engine caught at the first turn of the crank. That was a trick of the devil, for the engine died before we got out to the main road. My heart sank. I glanced at Bruce, with the crown and censer clasped in his arms, staring down the endless lane that disappeared in the lonely hills. Hallett's place was more than a mile and a half away, and the nearest turn of Route 90, with the thin chance of a lift, was more than two miles away.

Well, I thought, it's not tragically important. Bruce still said nothing, but his eyes were staring now at the big star twinkling just over the ragged edge of the mountain. Then an uneasy feeling stirred in me, because I knew the boy was praying. He had made his promise, too, and he was praying that nothing would keep him from being one of the Three Wise Men on this magic Christmas Eve.

I strained and heaved at the crank, but it was useless. I thought it over. When I looked up, Bruce was scuttling down the lane, one hand holding his skirts, the other swinging the censer, the high golden crown perched cockeyed on his head. I hesitated between laughing at him and yelling for him to stop. Then I began once more to crank.

Finally the engine coughed throatily. I scrambled into the car. Just about where the road enters town I overtook Bruce.

"You shouldn't have gone off that way," I growled. "It's too cold."

"I made a fire in the censer," he said. "I kept warm enough. I took a bearing on the star, made a short cut across Basoine's farm, and came out right by the new cottage." He shivered.

"But look at your feet! You might have frozen them!"

"It wasn't so bad."

We arrived at the school on time. I stood in back and watched. When I saw Bruce appear, walking stiff-legged on cut and chilblained feet, kneeling by the crèche declaiming his lines, I regretted my laughter at the dinner table. Then an uneasy awe rose up within me. Something stronger than a promise, I knew, had brought him through the bitter night to this sacred pageant.

Going home, Bruce showed me where the shortcut came out. "That's where the Thompsons live," he said, and added, "Harry Thompson died there."

As we passed the Basoine farm there were lights burning. I thought this was strange. Since George Basoine had gone off to war, the old grandmother, who had lost her youngest son in the first war, had sort of shriveled up, and a gloom lay over the house; but as I slowed down I could see Lou Basoine through the kitchen window, smoking his pipe and talking with his wife and mother.

That was about all there was to the evening. But on Christmas Day a friendly farmer's wife came by with gifts of mincemeat, made from venison, and a jug of sassafras cider. She went into the kitchen where my wife was supervising the Christmas feast. I drifted toward the kitchen, too, when I heard laughter there, since I have a weakness for the gossip of the countryside.

"You must hear this!" said my wife. The farmer's wife looked at me with a glittering but wary eye.

"You hain't a-goin' to believe it either," she said. "Just the same I'm tellin' you, folks up here in the hills see things and they do believe!"

"What have you been seeing?"

"It was old Mrs. Basoine. Last night when she was a-feelin' low she thought she heard something back of the barn and she looked out. Now I'll say this for the old lady—she's got good vision. There warn't no moonlight, but if you recollect it was a bright, starry night. And there she saw, plain as day, one of the Wise Men of the Bible come a-walkin' along the hill with a gold crown on his head, a-swingin' one of them pots with smoke in them—"

My wife and I looked at each other, but before I could say anything our visitor hurried on:

"Now don't you start a-laughin'. There's other testimony! Them Thompsons. You know the ones whose oldest boy died? Well, the children heard him first—a singin' 'Come, All Ye Faithful' plain as day. They went runnin' to the window, and they seen the Wise Man a-walkin' in the starlight across the lane, gold crown and robes, and fire pot and all!"

The farmer's wife looked defiantly at me. "Old folks and children see things that maybe we can't. All I can say is this: Basoines and Thompsons don't even know each other. But old lady Basoine was heartsick and lonely for her lost boy, and the Thompsons was heartsick and lonely because this was the first Christmas without Harry, and you dassent say they wasn't a-prayin' too! Maybe you don't believe that amounts to anythin' —but I'm tellin' you it was a comfort to them to see and believe!"

In the quiet of the kitchen the eyes of the two women searched my face—for disbelief, perhaps, since I'm not a very religious person. But whatever they expected, they were surprised at what they got.

I hadn't seen a vision that Christmas Eve, but what I had seen was to me far more impressive than any apparition: a flesh-and-blood small boy with a promise to keep, following over a trackless countryside the star which centuries ago led the Wise Men to Bethlehem. And it was not for me to deny the courage and the faith I saw in my son's eyes that night.

And so I said, with a sincerity which must have startled those two good women as much as it obviously pleased them:

"Yes, I believe that God is very close to us at Christmas."

Reprinted from the *Philadelphia Evening and Sunday Bulletin*, Philadelphia, Pennsylvania, December 24, 1942; as condensed in *Reader's Digest*, December 1945, pp. 1-3. Used by permission.

The Christmas We Gave Away

MARILYN ELLSWORTH SWINYARD

The Christmas I remember best began with tragedy. It happened at 6 A.M. on one of those crisp Idaho Falls mornings the day before Christmas. Our neighbors, the Jesse Smith family, slept peacefully in their two-story home. The baby, barely six months old, was in a crib next to her parents' room, and the three older children were upstairs.

Suddenly something jarred Jesse from his sleep. He thought he smelled smoke. Could a spark from the torch he'd defrosted the frozen water pipes with the day before have started a fire in the basement? Still half asleep, he stumbled to the bedroom door and flung it open. Clouds of black smoke poured into the room. "Lorraine!" he yelled. "Get the baby!" He ran toward the stairs and his sleeping children. The smoke was thicker as he gasped for breath. "Rick! Tom! Wake up!" The boys scrambled out of their beds. "Run, boys!" Tom grabbed his younger brother's hand, and they raced down the smoke-filled stairway to safety. His daughter's room was next. As Jesse groped through the heavy shroud of gray, he called, "Cindy! Cindy! Where are you?"

"Here, Daddy, here!" He followed the frightened cries, scooped up his daughter in his arms, and with his hand over her face, felt his way out the room and down through a narrow path of searing flames. They coughed, choked, gasped for breath, until they at last stumbled out the door where a relieved wife and three children stood shivering in the snow.

Now the family looked to the smoke and flames pouring out the roof of their home, the home that the night before had held all their earthly treasures. It had also held a promise of Christmas, mulled cider, homemade candy, and stockings waiting to be filled. They stood huddled in their nightclothes, barefoot in the biting cold, and watched their Christmas burn up along with their house.

The spell was broken by the sound of sirens piercing the icy air. Firemen leaped from the huge red trucks and turned their powerful hoses on the blaze. Seconds later, the bishop of the Smiths' ward drove up, bundled the family into his car, and took them to a home the ward elders quorum had just completed as a fund-raising project. They were not to witness the firemen's hopeless battle with the flames. For when the trucks finally pulled away, this time in silence, nothing stood of their house but its charred skeleton outlined against the sky.

And tomorrow was Christmas. At our house we were putting the last secret wrappings on the presents, making the last batch of popcorn for popcorn balls to go in our Christmas stockings. We three children were attempting dubious harmony with our favorite carols and breaking into giggles at the results.

Then Dad came in with the news. We sat with serious faces listening to him tell of the fire, the narrow escape, the house where the Smiths were spending Christmas Eve.

Why? Mother said. Why did this happen, just at Christmas? It isn't fair. They had children, just the same ages as ours, she said. Jesse and Dad were the closest friends; they even joked that they were so close they wore the same size shirt. The same size shirt! "Bill," Mother began hesitantly, "would you mind terribly if we gave Jesse one of the shirts I bought you for Christmas? You wear the same size . . ." A hush fell on us all. We all seemed to be thinking the exact same thing. "I've got it!" my ten-year-old brother shouted. "We'll give the Smiths a Christmas! A Christmas for Christmas!" "Where could we get one?" my inquisitive little sister asked. "We'll give them ours," the others chorused in.

"Of course! We'll give them ours!" The house rang with excited voices, until Dad's stern command silenced us. "Hold it! Let's make sure we all want to do this. Let's take a vote. All in favor say *aye.*"

"AYE!" chorused back at him. "All opposed?" was met with silence.

The hours that followed are ones we will never forget. First we sat around the tree and handed out presents. Instead of opening them, the giver would divulge their contents so the label could be changed to the appropriate Smith family member. My heart fell when Dad handed Kevin a box wrapped in gold foil and green ribbon. "It's a baseball glove, son," Dad told him, and a flash of disappointment crossed Kevin's face. I knew how he'd longed for that glove, and Dad wanted to say, "You keep it, son," but Kevin smiled as if he'd read our thoughts. "Thanks, Dad. It's just what Stan wanted, too," he replied.

"Look, here's the recipe holder I made for you, that is, for Sister Smith." We signed all the tags "From Santa," and the activity that followed would have put his workshop elves to shame.

They had presents, but what about a Christmas dinner? The turkey was cooked, pies baked, the carrots and celery prepared, and then all packed in a box. The Christmas stockings must be stuffed. Dad got a length of clothesline and some clothespins to hang the stockings with, but what about a tree? We looked at ours. Could we really part with it? "I know," Dad volunteered. "Let's decorate it with things they'll need." And so more things were added to the tree: a tube of toothpaste tied with red ribbon, a razor, comb, bars of soap nestled in the branches. Finally it was all ready.

It was a strange procession that silently paraded through the dark streets of Idaho Falls that night. Father led the way carrying a fully decorated tree. Mother followed with a complete Christmas dinner, down to the last dish of cranberry sauce. The three of us children pulled wagons and a sled piled with boxes of gifts. We waited until the last light was out in the Smiths' borrowed home, and then Mom and Dad stealthily carried each item in the door. When the last stocking had been hung, we turned again toward home.

All the way home I worried about what waited for my family at our home. What if the others were disappointed? All that was left were a few pine needles and paper scraps. I couldn't have been more wrong. The minute we were back inside we were more excited than ever. Every pine needle and paper scrap was a reminder of the magic of the evening, and we hadn't taken that to the Smiths. It was in our home as real as if you could see it. A happier family never went to bed on a Christmas Eve, and the next morning the magic was still there. For our celebration we wrote a promise to each person on a card and presented it around a spruce branch tied in a red ribbon.

"One shoe shine. To Father. Love Kevin." "This is good for two turns doing the evening dishes. Love, your husband Bill." And so it went.

Our Christmas dinner consisted of scrambled eggs and bacon, toast and sliced oranges. Somehow, I don't remember a better one. And I know we sang our caròls that night with the same unconventional harmony, but it sounded sweeter than angels to me.

"Oh, Mommy," said my small sister as she snuggled up for her bedtime Christmas story, "I like to give Christmases away." Tears blurred the book in my mother's hands, because she knew that none of us would ever forget this Christmas, the one when we gave our best gift. And as she read the story of the Baby born in a manger, it seemed our gift was but a small tribute to him who gave his best gift, his Son to us.

Deseret News, December 24, 1971, p. 1. Reprinted by permission. Marilyn Ellsworth Swinyard (Mrs. W. R.), who was born in Berkeley, California, was graduated from Brigham Young University. She has taught in Relief Society and the Sunday School. The Swinyards, who now reside in Palo Alto, California, have two children.

A Wonderful Christmas

WENDELL J. ASHTON

Christmas arrived some ten days early
for us that particular year. This is how it happened:

It had been a long and wearing day at the office, and I
phoned my wife Belva to call for me with her car.

Belva arrived in front of the office at about 6:30 P.M. The
sky was dark. The air was chilled. As I climbed into the little
light blue compact, Belva reminded me that we needed another
strand or two of small outdoor lights to decorate the oak trees
outside our dining room window.

"There is a little electrical store which may still be open,"
I said as we headed for the freeway. "Would you like to turn
back toward town, and I'll check at the store for some lights?"

Belva turned the car, and we were soon driving slowly
down a dark, narrow street not far from the building which
houses my office.

"There's the electrical store, down two or three doors," I
said, as we reached the intersection. I stepped out into the night
while Belva agreed to drive around the block.

As I moved toward the little white-fronted electrical store,
I noticed in the dark a man on the outside locking the door with
his keys. I hesitated to approach him. He no doubt had had a

long, hard day. I remembered clerking as a young man in a hardware store. We disliked having people knock on the windows and door after we had closed.

"May I help you?" the man spoke to me. His greeting surprised me. After all, I was a stranger in the night.

"I am looking for some strands of small Italian lights," I responded.

The man turned the key again and pushed open the door. "We have a rack with some of them," he said cheerily. "See, there are some, with little bell-shaped plastic holders for the individual lights."

The store was dark except for the area in which we stood. A gray-haired woman sat nearby sorting invoice slips. A man about seventy-five years of age joined us from the rear of the store. He greeted me by name. "For years I have had a special liking for you because of your father," he began. "Your father extended a kindness to my wife some thirty years ago. She was on a committee preparing a pioneer exhibit. He contributed materials for erecting a fence around the display, which included an old railroad engine, fire truck, and stagecoach."

The older man took me into his office in the rear of the store and proudly showed me some pictures on the wall of some of his family. We moved back near the display of Italian lights, and I completed the purchase of a box of the white lights on green strands.

"Give this man a special discount on those lights," the elderly gentleman said to the man who had opened the door, apparently his son.

As I turned to leave, the father called to me: "Will you wait a minute?" He moved to the rear of the store. Returning, he approached me. Then with his hand he grasped my tie. He placed a pearl-headed pin into my tie and fastened the pin.

"There," he added. "Have a merry Christmas, won't you!"

I choked a bit with tears as I moved out of the store into the darkness.

Tonight as I complete this little piece, I can see those bell-shaped Italian lights sparkling across the snow-covered oak boughs outside our window. I hope those lights never wear out.

They continue to remind me of a wonderful Christmas that began ten days early.

Instructor, December 1970. Brother Ashton, director of Public Communications for The Church of Jesus Christ of Latter-day Saints, is the author of seven books; for twenty-seven years he wrote a one-page feature that appeared on the back cover of the *Instructor* each month. He and his wife Belva have seven children.

First Christmas in Utah

LEVI EDGAR YOUNG

The first Christmas spent by the pioneers in Utah was one of thanksgiving. Food was scarce, and most of the people were housed in the Old Fort. While the winter was a mild one, there was intense suffering, especially among the women and children. There was a Christmas spirit on the twenty-fifth of December in the camp of the pioneers. There were no Christmas gifts as we have them today, but there was the larger thought of good will and mutual helpfulness. Everybody was ready to help and share. The finer instincts of religion and morals were manifested in clean thoughts and good deeds. Says one of the young girls of that day:

> I remember our first Christmas in the valley. We all worked as usual. The men gathered sagebrush, and some even plowed, for though it had snowed, the ground was still soft, and the plows were used nearly the entire day. Christmas came on Saturday. We celebrated the day on the Sabbath, when all gathered around the flagpole in the center of the fort, and there we held meeting. And what a meeting it was! We sang praise to God, we all joined in the opening prayer, and the speaking that day has always been remembered. There were words of thanksgiving and cheer. Not an

unkind word was uttered. The people were hopeful and buoyant because of their faith in the great work they were undertaking. After the meeting, there was handshaking all around. Some wept with joy, the children played in the enclosure, and around a sagebrush fire that night, we gathered and sang:

> Come, come ye Saints,
> No toil, nor labor fear,
> But with joy, wend your way.

That day, we had boiled rabbit and a little bread for our dinner. Father had shot some rabbits, and it was a feast we had. All had enough to eat. In the sense of perfect peace and good will, I never had a happier Christmas in all my life.

In the pioneer homes and towns of Utah, Christmas Day was always fittingly celebrated. And in those far-gone days, the children were taught to appreciate any little gift. There was no store full of toys, as we have them today. Sometimes a man gave a beaver skin or a buffalo robe to his wife and children. The gift made all happy. Often the head of a household provided venison and wild fowl for a feast, and all shared, and neighbors were invited to partake. There was no selfishness, no envy, no bigotry. People did not hold themselves aloof from others. There was a social equality and regard for one another that was sincere and spiritual. They were people who not only knew the truth, they were people of the truth. On Christmas Day, they had the real Christmas spirit. It was the day of Christ to them, and in every gift there was the expression of the love and good will of the giver. Children did not have every whim pacified; they were satisfied with any little plaything, and the dissatisfaction seen among the young people today was absent from the home and school. There was manifested a joy in living, and when they prayed they felt God's watchful care; when they worked, they knew of his helpful presence.

From Berta Huish Christensen, *Christmas Is for You* (Salt Lake City: Deseret Book Co., 1968), pp. 151-52. Levi Edgar Young was born February 2, 1874, in Salt Lake City, Utah. In 1910 he was called to the First Council of the Seventy in The Church of Jesus Christ of Latter-day Saints, and became senior member of that council in 1941. He died December 13, 1963.

Christmas Jewels for the Schoolmarm

MARIAN GARDNER NIELSON

nly a young, single schoolmarm could be as homesick as I was when I was stranded by the snow at Christmastime in southeastern Utah in 1926. Roads then were unpredictable, and the few autos around were even more unpredictable. I had planned on going home for the holidays, but an unprecedented snowstorm made travel impossible.

"Even if you could get out of here on the bobsleigh, you couldn't get those eighty miles to the train," argued the superintendent.

The mail got through once by sleigh. The mail sleigh for Blanding met the Monticello sleigh at Devil's Canyon, and first-class mail was exchanged. Then the steaming horses turned and floundered back over the steep, slippery road.

There was no other way out of town. But I was to experience one of the most unusual, one of the sweetest of Christmastimes. I was to actually feel what Christmas means.

It seemed that the whole town of Blanding had made up its collective mind that there was never to be one moment when I would have time to remember that this was my first Christmas away from home. They would prove that being snowed in could be a rewarding experience. The celebrating started as soon as school was out for the holidays.

Some of the older boys—who, by the way, were almost as old as I was—came to take me up to the reservoir to skate. Then Dee got a sled and pulled me through the streets behind his sorrel riding pony. Joe picked me up one morning in his sleigh and took me down to the field near Shirttail Corner to help feed the calves. It was slow going because the snow was so deep, but the warm rocks at our feet kept us comparatively comfortable. It was a thrilling sight for me to watch the Herefords trail in from the cedars when they heard the horses blowing.

During the crisp, snowy days, while being escorted around town or peering out through the store windows at the Redd Mercantile, I saw several sleighs, piled with cedar and pine cordwood, heading toward the Black Brothers flour mill and their homemade light plant. I counted the loads. I helped estimate the number of hours the wood could keep the light plant going. I knew that the size of the woodpile determined how many dances we could dance. Joe Huff was supposed to bring in several loads, but he had gone out to his traps beyond Westwater and no one knew when he would get back. So the whole town pitched in.

We had to have a Christmas tree for the Relief Society building and one for our boarding place at Aunt Martha's. Six of us bundled up, pulling on heavy, buckled galoshes, sweaters, and gloves, and went Christmas tree hunting.

I expected to sit on the sleigh and say "There's a beautiful pine over there" or "Whoa! There's the very cedar we want." But what happened? I was lifted out of the sleigh into the deep snow and told we couldn't possibly find a good tree so near the road. So I tramped and floundered and panted after the boys. I sprawled in hidden gullies and shivered with cold. All the trees I chose were either too scraggly, lopsided, bushy, uneven on one side, or not the right size. After two hours I was ready to settle for the next cedar or pine I saw. My galoshes were snow-packed, my woolen cap was hanging somewhere behind us on a cedar branch, my hands were blue with the cold, and I was wet from top to bottom. But what a beautiful day!

Joe finally saw a pine he thought was "pretty good." I was entranced with it. It was the right size and shape for our place, perfectly proportioned, complete with cones and bunches of mistletoe hanging from its branches. Then he cut a cedar tree studded thickly with blue cedar berries for the Relief Society building. No day could have been more perfect—wet clothes and all.

The services on the Sunday before Christmas Day were humble and sweetly reverent. The young bishop read the story of Jesus' birth from The Gospel According to Saint Luke. When he came to "For unto you is born this day in the city of David a Saviour, which is Christ the Lord," even the babies seemed to sense the holy stillness of that quiet stable.

All the nostalgic, unsophisticated old hymns were sung by a congregation made up of nearly every person in Blanding. Children were entranced with the age-old story; sweethearts resolved to keep the serenity of love in their own homes. Grandparents remembered past Christmas services on the red rocks above the Colorado River at the Hole-in-the-Rock, forty-six years before. And I, a schoolmarm, was encompassed by this rich love.

Two nights before Christmas half the town went caroling. Old, young, and middle-aged piled into sleighs and vied with the sleigh bells at every street corner. Glen had a couple of cowbells tied to his horses, but even they sounded subdued and mellow in the frosty air. We all sang lustily, our hearts full of laughter and reverence, our voices clear and strong. Along the way some persons waved from lighted windows, others from their front porches. And some brought out lighted lanterns to use in case the lights went out before we were through caroling. Because of the shortage of wood for the light plant at the mill, Uncle Edson would wink the lights at 9:30, half an hour before he shut them off. We all knew we had only that limited time, so we had either to dash home and get settled in bed before ten or have enough lamps and lanterns to light our late festivities.

Uncle Edson waited until the carolers were at the little Relief Society hall before he winked the lights. We all hurried to get everything on the tables. It was a noisy group, but when the oyster soup and crackers were placed on the trestle tables, the carolers quieted down like magic. Platte had a race with Ed Stevens to see who could eat the most soup, so some of us didn't even get any.

Coasting was something else again! The snow had stopped falling, and that great big round yellow moon standing high over Ute Mountain brightened up the downhill coast run. There was a sharp turn at the bottom of the hill. Miss Gordon missed the turn and landed headfirst in the deep snow in the creek bottom. We didn't find her sled until the next day. Lloyd had borrowed his father's watch so he could tell what time to leave for the dance. He wanted to make the longest run down the hill and win the prize: escorting the schoolmarms home after the dance. He lay flat on his stomach, gave a shove with his feet, and flew down the slide. He made the longest run, all right, but he hit the third bump near the big cedar so hard that he smashed the watch to smithereens. He wasn't even interested in taking anyone home after that. He didn't even want to go home.

Christmas Eve was family night. I was invited to nearly every home in town, but I stayed at Aunt Martha's, filling stockings, wrapping gifts I had made, singing carols with the family, peeking out to see if Joe and Junior were going to sneak in for a few minutes. I watched Aunt Martha make her famous Boston creams. I helped pop a big dishpan full of popcorn. (Somehow it seemed the kernels popped whiter, larger, and were more tender than are those of today. I wonder why.) When Joe knocked on the kitchen door and handed Aunt Martha two gaily wrapped, bulky packages with strict orders for me not to open them until morning, my Christmas Eve was complete.

And then at last it was Christmas Day. A steady stream of people came to see what the schoolmarms got for Christmas and to bring other gifts. All of Miss Gordon's male students brought gifts to her, from tiny bottles of perfume to gay calico sacks filled with pinion nuts and pine gum. My gifts, mostly from female students, were crocheted pot holders and doilies and a Ute-woven reed basket that I adored. Such homemade candy, such talking and such silences, such hearty Christmas wishes and friendliness and goodwill as filled that little house!

But the climax, of course, was the Christmas dance. There had been a dance every night, even after the Home Dramatics Club presentation of East Lynn. But this dance was something special. It was held in the recreation center in the basement of the church. Everyone went: babies, children, adolescents, adults, and the schoolteachers. The hall was fragrant with the scent of pine and cedar boughs. Even sprigs of sagebrush hung in the windows. Huge balls of mesa mistletoe were suspended from the pipes along the ceiling. The stage had a gigantic Christmas tree, lighted the first time at this dance.

Young mothers brought quilts and pillows and settled their babies and small children in the furnace room on improvised beds.

Lutie Harris played the piano and Hyrum Porter the fiddle. The music brought everyone onto the floor. There was no dancing with just the partner you came with, no standing in one place all evening. This was real dancing.

Uncle Kumen and Aunt Mary, seventy years young, waltzed nimbly around the hall, despite Aunt Mary's lame leg. Young Riley Hurst gallantly led his beautiful black-haired mother onto the dance floor. Andrew Peterson and his Viola, grandparents from way back, two-stepped blithely up and down the hall.

High school student Glen, with Eva, his steady, kicked up his heels. The whole audience enjoyed their dancing. Two youngsters from Bluff got a great deal of applause for their fancy steps and easy rhythm. Uncle Zeke, the colorful guide at the Natural Bridges, asked me for a set and we won first prize for the best waltzing couple.

One of the earnest young male dancers complained at the rough floor and demanded that the janitor put more wax on it. We laughed and laughed when we saw he was still wearing his rubber galoshes.

Of course, we had to get off the floor once or twice during the evening so the janitor could sweep it, but there were many eager helpers, and it didn't take long.

So everyone danced. Everyone laughed and enjoyed everyone's company. Democrats forgot that their Republican neighbors were enemies. Vernon and Kim, courting the same girl, were actually seen laughing together. The proprietors of the two stores sat out two sets and calmly discussed who turned out the best beef for their customers. It was a gala occasion. It was real fun. It was a time of rejoicing—Christmas.

When the lights winked at 11:30, Aunt Mary limped out, urging Uncle Kumen, "Hurry now, Kumen, before the rush starts."

But the rush had already started. With just half an hour to get home before darkness enveloped the community, the hall was soon cleared. Sleighs were drawn up before the church for the older couples; a few horses were tied to the fence across the street. Most people trudged up the middle of the road, all quieter now but calling "Goodnight" and "Merry Christmas" to everyone.

Joe and I walked up the road too, and I felt blessed to have been a part of such a joyous, satisfying Christmas. The simple joys of friendship, graciousness, thoughtfulness, and thank-God-fulness were all combined to make a schoolmarm feel wanted and accepted. It was truly a Christmas of sharing.

Ensign, December 1971, pp. 21-23. Marian Gardner Nielson and her husband, Joseph L. Nielson, have seven children. Sister Nielson, a resident of Blanding, Utah, who taught high school English for fourteen years, wrote many stories, poems, plays, and pageants and was co-author of a book. She was the 1967 Utah State Mother of the Year. She died November 25, 1972.

Twice Blest

HELEN ROMRELL

Ann sat at her desk—usually letters were so easy to write, but today was different. Christmas was almost here, but with all the excitement and preparations, Ann still felt a little apprehensive—how would Steve, her firstborn, spend Christmas this year? Germany was such a long way from Idaho, and even though he was completely absorbed in his missionary work, she still worried about him. This would be his first Christmas away from home. She knew he would miss his brothers and sister and the happiness they all shared at this special time of year.

Well, she must hurry if she was to catch the postman and still make it to Relief Society on time.

Smiling now, she quickly added messages from the younger children and encouagement and love from all. She reread the letter and was sure that it did not betray her feelings.

As she stepped out the door to put her letter in the box, she met the postman coming up the walk. He smiled as he saw her scanning the letters in his hand, looking for the familiar blue aerogramme.

Cheerfully they exchanged greetings and Ann hurried inside. She sat down in the easy chair and slowly opened the

precious letter, for she savored this moment. It was almost like
hearing Steve's voice as she read his words, and a smile filled her
face.

The spell was soon broken as she looked at the clock. She
had better hurry or Sister Adams would think she wasn't coming
to pick her up.

Later, seated in the cozy Relief Society room, decked out in
Christmas finery today, her mind went back to the letter, as she
listened to the music and waited for the meeting to begin.

Wasn't it just too wonderful! Steve wouldn't be spending
Christmas alone after all. In his letter he had told of a wonderful family who had invited him to share their Christmas with
them. Her heart was full of gratitude as she thought of this unknown nonmember family who were giving—giving a gift of love
—wasn't that what the lesson brought out today?

As the social relations lesson, "A City on a Hill," with its
beautiful message of Chrismas unfolded, Ann again felt grateful
to those who had true love in their hearts and were willing to
share.

The lesson was finished all too soon—Ann hated to break the
magical spell, and was engrossed in her own thoughts as she heard
Sister Wright say, "If anyone wishes to give a true gift of love
this holiday season, I know a girl at college who is most deserving.
She is from the East and cannot go home for Christmas. She will
be all alone this season."

Ann's heart pounded. She could hardly wait for the meeting
to close. Would this be her chance to repay those unknown
friends by giving a gift of love to another one in need?

Quickly she found Sister Wright. "We would love to share
our Christmas with the girl you mentioned—tell me more about
her."

The Wrights had made it a tradition to extend their Christmas beyond the normal limits of family and close friends, and
this year as they were planning their special project, they had
asked the help of a professor at college. He surely would know
someone who needed help. With his assistance, they had made
their plans, but today as Sister Wright had listened to the lesson
Linda's name kept coming to mind.

Linda was one of the girls Professor Wilson had told them about while discussing possible projects, and now she told Linda's story to Ann.

Linda was very shy and had a difficult time looking people in the eye. She went around with her head down most of the time. Her parents sold stovewood for a living. Her mother wrote to her often and expressed her love for her, but her father never wrote. He seemed to resent her coming west for school, perhaps because he felt he could not help her as he should. She had worked to earn her own money to go to school. She was withdrawn, but courageous. She surely needed a gift of love!

The arrangements were made and Ann and her whole family anxiously awaited Linda's arrival.

A very small, shy, frightened girl came up the walk in a shapeless coat, carrying a very small suitcase and wearing a well-worn, drab, plain, green dress.

It wasn't long until she responded to the warmth and the love of the family. She had no brothers, and Ann's four boys were a new experience to her in family living. She loved the baby! Ann and Linda got along well, and a close relationship soon developed between them.

The following Sunday the bishop asked all of the students home for the holidays to bear their testimonies and tell about their schools. As he called on Linda, he explained she was a convert of only two years and was a guest in the ward. Would she care to respond?

It took a great deal of courage for Linda to respond with her sweet, humble testimony, and the hearts of the ward members were touched.

On the following Wednesday Linda went to Relief Society with Ann and met many of the sisters in the ward. Again she wore the plain green dress, the only dress she had brought with her for a two-weeks' visit!

Ann took Linda shopping, and together they picked out some lovely woolen material, and Ann made her a beautiful wool dress, the first wool dress she had ever owned. How thrilled she was!

Not long afterwards, Sister Wright called. She wanted to do

something for Linda, too. Would she like to go shopping for a new coat?

Linda was hesitant at first, but soon warmed to the graciousness of Sister Wright. It was a radiant, happy girl who returned home that evening in a most becoming red coat.

Linda left Ann's home on Christmas Eve to spend the night and part of Christmas Day with her roommate in a nearby town. They had wanted to be together, and these were the only two days they could accommodate her.

As she left, her arms were full of gaily wrapped packages, gifts from many members of the ward. No one had organized a plan, no one spread the word of her need, but many families had sensed her need and individually responded with a gift of love for this sweet girl!

On Christmas morning things were not quite the same at Ann's home. The family was excited opening their gifts, but something was missing! But not for long—suddenly the telephone rang. It was Linda! She was thinking of them, missing them, and wanting to share the excitement of this very special Christmas with them.

"Perhaps the best gift of all," Linda's voice broke, "I just received a letter from my father! My very first! And he sent me ten dollars, and more important, for the first time that I can remember, he told me that he loves me."

Ann's eyes were full of tears as she put the telephone down. She turned and walked away from the family noise and into Linda's room.

"Here I thought I was doing something for someone, helping someone else, and it is I who have been blessed!" Ann whispered.

_____

Relief Society Magazine, November 1968, pp. 837-39. Helen Romrell and her husband, Milton Romrell, reside in Idaho Falls, Idaho; they have six sons and a foster daughter. Sister Romrell has served in ward and stake capacities in auxiliaries of the Church.

Special Package for You Today

RANETTA VAN ZYVERDEN

The Christmas I remember best was but a few years ago. I had been away from home, working and going to school for the past few years. But the year of my experience was different. I had married and was blessed with a two-month-old son. My husband was going to college and working all night to bring in a meager income. Yet we had managed to purchase a humble Christmas tree that to us was tall in stature. As I sat looking upon its bare limbs I reflected on past Christmases.

There I was home in Kansas, where I was reared by my grandparents. How I loved those specially adorned Christmas trees with sparkling ornaments of history. We would cut down our own cedar tree.

After setting it up at home, we would drag out that old heavy cardboard box which held the trimmings. Decorating was always my treat, taking out the familiar items, some being very old, saved off trees of my great-great-grandmother's. I cherished those little things, like the little glass angel that spun from a string. Another was a little china doll my father had received as a child at a Christmas party. It still wore the same ribbon dress. My father had passed on when I was only five, so it was very dear to me.

In this collection was a set of lights, much older than I, of different animals, plus the old metal reflectors to put behind the regular lights, some made to add to the set. There were strings of glass beads over sixty years old. And then there were those two very short strings more than a hundred years old— short because so many of them had been broken. I was grateful they were saved and handed down. A special small box held carefully wrapped ornamental balls that were fragile with age.

There were new things, too, that had been bought when I was a little girl, which we had also added each year. Probably the best-loved by me was the face of an angel with a light behind. I had chosen a blue light to put behind her more than any other color through the years. It always gave her a peaceful and soft glow. Last, but not least, when everything was on, we finished by drenching the tree with icicles. We would turn off all the house lights, turn on the tree lights, and just sit and look at it. Often friends or neighbors would be there to witness the first lighting.

It seemed as though we had for a short time caught up and captured all the Christmases from years and years ago. We had a glimpse of something someone else in some other time had enjoyed, and now we were privileged to share it. There it was, glittering, shining, regal, elegantly dressed, reigned over by an angel face in a star.

As I was remembering these wonderful things a sadness filled my heart. Tears welled up in my eyes. I knew we could hardly afford the tree, let alone anything to go on it. The tears streamed down my face as I looked at our little son. I'm being foolish; he won't even remember this Christmas. Still it was his first Yuletide and my tears kept coming.

How I wish we could have done more. At that moment the doorbell rang.

"Who on earth. . . ?" I muttered as I went to the door, trying to wipe away my tears.

"Special package for you today," greeted a smiling postman. "Sign here, please."

I signed, and as he stepped back he handed me a box. "Gifts from home," I thought. "Great. Well, at least we'll have gifts to go under our tree."

As I pulled away the brown paper wrapping there was that familiar old cardboard box, and there was a letter on top which read:

"My dear child, I thought you would like to have these. Dad and I are too old and will not be putting up eight and nine foot trees anymore. I know that it is hard starting out in life. I know that you always loved the things we had and that they have a special meaning to you. Our love and best wishes for your happiness, Mom and Dad. P.S. Have a Merry Christmas."

As I took out and looked at the cherished items, my tears were tears of joy! It wasn't long until my loving husband came in from school, and together we decorated our first tree. When we had finished we sat down and turned it on. It was as though we had lit the memory of all the years gone by. Surely the same spirit that brought joy into the lives of those throughout other years was now being shared by us. Our little son stared in wonder at so many different colored lights as I slipped into my husband's arms. We looked out and thick flakes of snow were falling. This was truly the best Christmas.

Deseret News, December 21, 1972, p. 1. Reprinted by permission. Ranetta Van Zyverden, a native of San Bernardino, California, is married to Sjors C. A. Van Zyverden. They are parents of three children, and the family presently resides in Denver, Colorado.

Pink Dresser

WENDELL J. ASHTON

Tonight as I look out of our living room window on the city below, the bright Christmas lights on the homes have almost totally vanished in the quiet of falling snow. When the night sky was clear, the city looked like a vast, glittering jewel box.

I have been reflecting on the Christmases in my life through more than half a century.

One of the most memorable was one which did not affect me personally very much at the time. But it has through the years.

This is the story, as I recall it:

My father managed a building supply business at the time. Our home was a two-story, brown-red brick house with a steep roof, on the outskirts of town. My two younger sisters occupied a bedroom on the second floor. One sister was about nine years old; the other, six. From their bedroom windows they looked down on our garage and driveway below.

My father and mother had made their plans for their two younger daughters' Christmas. Each would receive a beautiful pink dresser, with a mirror and several drawers. There was a cabinetmaker near my father's business who would be asked to make the play dressers.

The cabinetmaker began his work.

As Christmas neared, the two blonde sisters talked hopefully about what they might receive on that most wonderful morning of the year. Dolls? A pair of skates for one, a sled for the other? A new dress or a nightgown? A game for family fun or a set of play dishes?

Christmas Eve arrived. It was a night when we six children slept little. My father's car rolled into the driveway in the dark. When the door of the car opened, the two wide-eyed little girls pressed their noses against their window over the driveway. They saw something pink in or on the car. Excitedly, they returned to their beds.

It was the practice in our home on Christmas morning for the children to form a line, then move on a signal from Mother into the living room. Here was the Christmas tree. Gifts were placed on and near chairs about the room.

Between two of the chairs there was a pink dresser with gleaming mirror. There was the sweet aroma of pine wood and fresh paint. The dresser even smelled good.

But there was only one dresser.

My mother drew the two sisters to her side. Almost tearfully she explained:

"There were two pink dressers, one for each of you. But last night your father thought of a widow's family. He wondered what kind of Christmas they would have. She has two daughters, too. Your father decided to take one of the pink dressers to their home. This one here this morning is for you two girls to share."

They did share it in their bedroom for some fifteen years. They played with it together. One placed her handkerchiefs and stockings in one of its drawers. The other sister kept hers in another drawer.

That Chrismas was some forty years ago. My sisters, each with a family of her own now, still share the pink dresser. Their daughters share it, too. Their mothers have told the girls the story of why it is special.

For some years the pink dresser has been in a playhouse in the basement of one of my sisters' homes. It has been there when we have gathered at Christmas time.

"We two sisters have been so close through the years," one

of them said to me recently. "That pink dresser has helped bring us even closer—and our children, too."

The pink dresser has done something for me and my children. So has the other pink dresser. It continues to remind me that some of the things we enjoy most in life are those which we have given up.

Instructor, December 1968.

Christmas Remembered

BERTA HUISH CHRISTENSEN

he Christmas I remember best introduced me to the wonder-world of the Christmas tree. Before this memorable morning, the traditional evergreen, with its tinseled branches, was to my young mind only for story books.

Our little town was situated in a wide, semidesert valley in northern Mexico. The mountains to the west were miles away; eastward, the prairie swept in unbroken grassland to the more distant hills, so that Christmas trees in this pioneer community were not a common item. Sometimes our boxed gifts would be arranged in pyramid form, resembling a tree, and placed on the dining table with its bright red tablecloth. Or they might be grouped around the stockings which hung from the bedpost or, perhaps, the back of a chair.

There was the aroma of parched and popped corn, of holiday cookery—pie and gingerbread. The cookies, which we all helped to make, would be shared with small Mexican children who always came around on Christmas morning. We were accustomed to a dry-ground Christmas, but on this particular Christmas Eve there was a very light snowfall. One of the children spoke of it as soapsuds.

Before dawn (who could sleep longer?) we filed downstairs

to the dining room, my brother carrying the lighted lamp. We were in long outing-flannel nightgowns, and our feet were bare. The parlor door was closed. Mama insisted that we put our stockings on and that we wait in the dining room for a few minutes. We were breathless with excitement. Then the parlor door opened and my father and eldest sister came out to usher us in, youngest ones first. There before my eyes was a sight I had never seen before—even more wonderful than in the storybooks. A beautiful green Christmas tree standing in the middle of the room like a tree of stars!

It was a large tree, its top almost touching the high ceiling. There were no fancy ornaments, just shining red apples suspended by thread, and there were strings of popcorn. Nestling in the branches were three beautiful dolls. Their eyes would open and close, their heads were breakable, they had curly hair, and they wore little black slippers. I recall that my doll wore a shiny red cambric dress with a pleated skirt.

Most beautiful of all were the twinkly lighted candles. They were in small metal holders, clipped to the branches. There were lots of them—blue candles, white candles, red candles. We gasped "Oh!" and Ah!" and then we fairly shouted, dancing 'round and 'round the tree. The dance was brief, for the life of the candle was brief, and there was danger of fire. The older girls, standing on chairs, blew out the higher lights; we younger children puffed out those within our reach.

I recall that there were wrapped and ribbon-tied boxes at the base of the tree, but I do not recall what the presents were. No one thought much about gifts, the tree was so beautiful. To this day I cannot cover the beauty of the Christmas tree with innumerable baubles.

I do not know how my parents came by that tree. Children do not ask; that is part of the mystery of Christmas. Since then I have not thought to inquire. But from this first Christmas tree has come my aesthetic appreciation of the evergreen as part of the Christmas scene.

We have purchased and I have trimmed beautiful trees— pine from the woods of upper New York, fir from the forests of New Hampshire, blue spruce from the Canadian Rockies, and pinon pine from our western states, but I believe that no tree will ever diminish the aura of wonder that surrounds that first Christmas tree with its full green branches, its starry, twisted little Mexican candles, burning with so brief a light, yet with a radiance lasting through the years.

Berta Huish Christensen, *Christmas Is for You* (Salt Lake City: Deseret Book Co., 1968), pp. 160-61. Sister Christensen, who has written many articles, poems, dramatic programs, and lessons, and has won several writing awards, is a member of the Relief Society general board.

And a Merry Christmas to Everyone

J. ARTHUR HORNE

Attorney James Brown stood on the sidewalk of Sixth Avenue and gazed at the half-finished structure which was to be his home. Busy workmen were engaged with hammer and trowel on various parts of the building, while great piles of brick and stone, lumber, and shining slabs of marble were strewn about the grounds indicating the palatial nature of this modern dwelling. While the lawyer stood there enjoying this scene of activity a smile overspread his handsome features. This was the fulfilment of one of his dreams—to have one of the finest homes in the city. . . .

A man in a dark suit, evidently the architect in charge, came out of the building and joined the lawyer on the sidewalk.

"Billings, I have to leave for the coast this afternoon. The Oil Lands case has been called for the first week in October, and I'm not half ready. I will probably be gone all winter."

"We'll not be through here before the latter part of April, anyway, Mr. Brown, so you'll likely be back before we finish the interior," replied the architect. "The city department gave us the house number this morning. It is 914."

"Don't slight anything, Billings, even if it goes a little over the estimate. A man builds only one house like this in a lifetime."

The same morning that this incident occurred another James Brown also stood on the sidewalk in front of his home. He, too, was going away to try his fortune in another state. Thus far success had eluded him. . . .

"Don't worry, Alice, I'll be back safe and sound, never fear. Kiss Jamie and Winnie and Ted for me when they come home from school."

Alice turned to her household duties with a heavy heart. She loved her husband dearly and missed him when he went away. In their earlier married life she had accompanied him to several of the camps where he worked as an assayer, but since the children were old enough to attend school she had been compelled to stay at home.

Jim's first letter from Nevada told of a change in his plans. "I've decided to take a lease," he wrote. "There's a fine fellow here named Bill Stauffer who will go with me. The mining company agrees to furnish transportation to the railroad for our ores at the same rate they pay for their own. I see no reason why we shouldn't clean up a bunch of money." . . .

By spring Jim figured they had nearly $20,000 worth of ore stored in the tunnel. . . .

A few days later Alice beheld a blue-coated messenger boy dismount from his bicycle in front of her house and come up the walk. With trembling fingers she signed for the telegram and hastened into her bedroom to read it:

Lone Pine Mountain, Nevada, May 19, 1920

Mrs. James Brown
914 Sixth East St., City.

Jim injured hauling ore. Will reach city four-thirty today.
Wm. Stauffer.

Alice crushed the telegram in her hands and offered a silent prayer that Jim's injuries would not prove serious. . . .

When the train pulled in, Alice was standing with the children on the platform, and when it came to a stop she eagerly scanned the car exits for sight of her husband. Presently she saw the white-coated driver of the ambulance approach one of the cars and she hurried over to him. . . .

The children began to cry when they saw their father lying there so limp and helpless.

. . . The next morning's paper which contained among the local items a brief account of Jim Brown's accident had blazoned forth on the front page a picture of the state's noted lawyer James Brown and an accompanying article telling of his success in winning the first of his Oil Land cases in California.

At last the day came when the cast was removed and Jim once more stood upon his feet. . . .

Throughout all this trying period Alice's faith and trust in God had never wavered, but now it seemed as if all things conspired together to break her spirit. When Jim left the hospital he entered the great army of unemployed who walked the streets of our cities from the fall of 1920 until the spring of 1922. Mines were closing down or running only part-time; stores and factories were cutting their forces; building was almost at a standstill; and gaunt poverty and distress were on every hand. The twelve hundred dollars which Jim had received as his portion of the mining venture was about exhausted when his hospital and doctor bills were paid. Still their hearts were brave when they returned to their humble home on Sixth East, and Jim set out early the next morning to try and find employment.

The first person he encountered was Joe Sanders, a brother assayer. "Still with the King Company, Joe?" Jim asked.

"No, they closed down two months ago. Didn't you know?"

"I hadn't heard. I've been in the hospital, so I guess I'm not up on the latest news. What are you driving at now?"

"Hunting another job," Joe answered. "And you?"

"Same thing. Are jobs really that scarce?"

"I'll say they are." They wished each other luck and passed on. Jim called in at several assay offices where he was well-known, and in each of them he found men seeking employment. At first he was not discouraged. He was a good assayer and had never before experienced any difficulty getting a position. As the days wore on, however, the full extent of the mining collapse became apparent.

"I guess I'll have to find some other kind of work," he told Alice. . . .

It grew colder, and he turned his footsteps home.

Alice tried to greet him with a smile when he opened the

door, but when she saw the drawn look on his face she burst into tears. He put his arm about her and led her to a chair in the kitchen. The children had placed the broom across the backs of two chairs, and hanging suspended from it were four stockings of varying lengths. "It wouldn't be so bad for us," Alice sobbed on his shoulder, "we could stand it, but the children—not a thing in the house for their Christmas. Whatever in the world are we going to do, Jim?" He was about to speak when their attention was arrested by a quick step on the back porch and a hurried thump on the door. Jim got up and opened the door. A young fellow in overalls and jumper smeared with flour confronted them.

"Is this number 914?" he asked. Jim nodded assent. "We've brought your groceries; where'll we put 'em?"

"I didn't order any groceries," Jim answered. "You must have the wrong number."

"Ain't your name Brown, James Brown?" the young fellow persisted, looking at a paper in his hand.

"Yes," Jim answered, puzzled.

"This is the place all right. We'll back in." He dashed off into the darkness, and the next moment they heard the chug of a motor. The rear end of a big truck loomed out of the darkness and bumped into the porch. Two men began piling things onto the porch. Sacks of flour, potatoes, and sugar; cases of soap, canned milk, fruit, and vegetables; boxes, bundles, and packages of every description were unceremoniously dumped onto the porch or carried into the kitchen, while the bewildered family stood about in utter amazement. When a pretty Christmas tree appeared, the silence was suddenly broken by cries and exclamations of delight from the children, and the tree was carried triumphantly into the front room.

"Who sent all this?" Jim finally asked one of the men.

"I dunno, Mister; Santa Claus, I reckon." The next minute the two men climbed into their truck and rode off into the night.

Jim and Alice looked into each other's faces questioningly. Jim was the first to speak. "Who in the world could have sent them?"

"It must have been Bill Stauffer," she answered. "He sent a

card saying he would see us at Christmas time. You see, he had twelve hundred dollars from the lease, the same as we did."

Jim shook his head. "No, Alice, the check he sent us was the total received from our ore. I saw a copy of the account while I was out at the smelter. The big-hearted fellow kept not one cent for himself. No, it must have been someone else."

Still mystified, they began to look over the things. A box of brilliant-colored trimmings came first into view. These were seized upon by the children and carried into the front room where Jamie was already setting up the tree. Alice next uncovered two beautiful dolls and hastily hid them in her bedroom. Doll carriages, a tricycle, books, games, and toys were quickly hidden away. Candies, nuts, oranges, and apples followed. A turkey she laid on the table. By this time Alice was in a perfect delight. "I just knew the Lord would not forsake us!" she said.

But Jim still felt that all was not right. At first he had been stunned by this sudden change from poverty to affluence, but now he began to collect his scattered wits. He went out onto the porch and looked the things over. With a sickening sensation the truth suddenly dawned on him; this was undoubtedly the supply Attorney Brown had ordered for his own home. Someone at the store had blundered. Instead of delivering the things to Sixth Avenue they had been brought to Sixth East. He remembered now the house number was 914—the same as his. An error such as this would probably not occur in any other city in the United States. "Of course the mistake will be discovered as soon as Attorney Brown reaches his home and finds the things have not been delivered. He'll call the store, and the things will be traced to us. Anyway, I'll have to notify the store. These things are not meant for us at all."

Shout of joyous laughter came to him from the house and pierced his heart like knife thrusts. "My poor little kids," he exclaimed, "I'm afraid your joy will be short-lived." With a groan he sat down on one of the boxes and covered his face with his hands. "And Alice, my dear, sweet wife! It will nearly break her heart when she learns the truth." Tears welled up into his eyes.

How long he sat thus he did not know. He was roused by the

sound of an automobile stopping in front of the house. He got up and walked over beyond the edge of the building and peered out. In the darkness he made out the figure of a man just stepping from an automobile. "It's all over," he said to himself in a choking voice, "all over." He leaned against the porch post to steady himself for a minute or two, and then went slowly into the house.

When he reached the door that opened into the front room he swung it open unnoticed and stopped within the shadow. Just inside the front door, hat in hand, stood Attorney Brown. Ted had evidently let him in, for Alice with flushed face and shining eyes was coming out from behind the gaily decorated tree. She stared in astonishment at seeing the unexpected visitor. "Well, how-d-you-do?" she greeted him cheerily.

"I ordered some things sent—sent—," the lawyer began awkwardly. Alice advanced toward him.

"Are you the one who so generously sent us these things?" she asked in amazement. He blinked his eyes a couple of times and appeared to swallow something.

"A—a—, yes, ma'am." Alice went to him and took his hand in both of hers.

"God bless your kind heart," she said fervently, and there were tears in her eyes when she said it. "I don't know who you are, but I know that Providence sent you to us in our time of need. You cannot know what it means to go day after day, month after month without employment, never knowing one day what you will have to eat the next. Surely God put it in your heart to do this noble deed." She released his hand, and he shifted his weight awkwardly from one foot to the other.

"I'm afraid you are giving me more credit than I deserve," he replied. Then a merry twinkle came into his eyes and he smiled good-humoredly. "I thought I'd just take a run down and see if the things were delivered all right."

Jim was struggling to adjust himself to the unexpected turn the case had taken. He advanced into the room, extending his hand, which the other took in a hearty handshake. "I don't know how to thank you, but I'll repay you as soon as I can get to earning again." The attorney laid his hand on Jim's shoulder.

"Now, don't talk about paying me, nor thanking me, either,

or you'll spoil it all. This is the first time in my life I've ever been a real Santa Claus." He looked at the children playing about the tree, talking in suppressed excited tones, their hearts almost bursting with joy. Never had they dreamed of a Christmas like this. The scene evidently touched the heart of the great lawyer, for he took the chair Alice offered him and sat for some time gazing at them in silence. "My!" he finally exclaimed, "I wouldn't have missed this for a thousand dollars." He arose and turned to Jim.

"Let's see, you say you are out of employment, Mr.—Mr.—.

"Brown, the same as yours," Jim answered. The lawyer looked startled for a moment.

"Oh—, oh yes, I see. What is your occupation, Mr. Brown?" Jim told him. "Assayer? Good! My brother-in-law is superintendent of the smelter." He took a card from his pocket and handed it to Jim. "If you'll call at my office any time after tomorrow I'll give you a letter to him. He'll find a place for you. Well, I must be going. I've a few purchases to make before the stores close." He bowed gracefully to Alice. "Good-night," he said, then sweeping the room with his glance added, "and a Merry Christmas to everyone."

"Merry Christmas! Merry Christmas!" chorused after him as he closed the door.

The parents looked at each other in silence for a moment, and then Alice put her arms around her husband's neck and drew his face down to hers. "Now, will you say the Lord isn't watching over us?" she challenged.

And he answered, "I wouldn't dare."

Improvement Era, December 1923, pp. 115-25. Note: This story is fiction.

The Widow's Might

ELAINE S. McKAY

Bessie watched the wind hurl snow as it howled through Huntsville. It's a cold Christmas Eve, she thought . . . colder than those of the Depression . . . colder now that her husband was dead.

Before the fire had flickered out, Bessie had heated the iron and made her way up the winding stairs of the stone home to iron the sheets before her eight children climbed into their beds. "Warmmm," purred the baby as she snuggled in her crib. Even Bessie's sixteen-year-old son chuckled and sighed as his feet found where the iron had been. The children were noisily unaware that the iron was heated by bits of slack coal from a supply that wouldn't last the winter. Nor had they ever noticed that the smiling woman who pressed the sheets wore patched dresses and was somehow never hungry.

The next morning Bessie would build the fire while the four boys went out to feed and milk old Sally, the only animal not sold to pay debts. The little girls would wait in the kitchen until chores were done. Then all would line up—smallest to tallest—and, at the sound of Bessie's first notes on the piano, would march and sing their way in to the tree. . . . "O come, all ye faithful, joyful and triumphant. . . ."

They had cut the tree themselves and trimmed it with paper chains and popcorn. But there was nothing under it, and Bessie had little to put there. She had bought oranges and nuts. That was enough, she knew, to cause shouts of delight. But, as she sat looking out at the half-buried village the old question returned, "What can I give my children for Christmas?" After a moment, she saw the answer.

In the morning when songs were sung and oranges eaten, Bessie said, "Today, because it's Christmas day, we're going to do something special. We are going to take gifts to a family who are poor." The house grew quiet. *Poor* was a word they shunned.

Then Bessie, her eyes shining, explained that many people in the world had very little and since they themselves had so much it was only right that they share. They could look through their possessions and find a gift—a hair ribbon, a book, some clothes. . . . "And I'll make apple pies," she beamed.

When the pies were cooled, Bessie placed two in a basket where the children had put their gifts. She covered all with a bright cloth. At last everything was ready. Then, above the excited chatter, a boy's voice demanded, "Mother, why are we doing this when we don't have enough for ourselves?"

There. Someone had said it. The smiles vanished. Even the baby was silent.

"What we have is enough," Bessie said softly, "and what we are giving is small. We are keeping the precious things . . . our testimonies of the gospel, this great stone house built by your grandfather, our love for each other, happy memories of what has been, hope for good things that are to come. . . . All this is ours to keep. These few gifts we have gathered are ours to share. . . . Come, my son, you may carry the basket."

Christmas night was cold, and Bessie again ironed the sheets. Amid the clamor of getting ready for bed, she felt a sense and assurance. She could not know that one of her sons would become a United States Congressman, that all of them would fill missions and serve their country in foreign lands. She could not visualize the twelve college degrees, the scholarships, trophies, and awards that her sons and daughters would accumulate. Nor could she know for sure that each would marry in a temple. She could not foresee the shared planning, pennies, and prayers that would cause it all to happen. And later that evening as she watched the last embers die in the old stove and felt the house grow more cold, she little knew that in twenty-seven years she would be named Utah's Mother of the Year.

Bessie knew only that she had given her children something for Christmas that they could never lose. Years from now on a cold winter night when they were far from home, they would find it, small and sacred, in their hearts. And there would be other things she could give to them as days and months went by—little things—like warmed sheets.

Relief Society Magazine, December 1970, pp. 898-99. Elaine S. McKay is the wife of Salt Lake City attorney Bàrrie Gunn McKay; they are the parents of five children. A successful free-lance writer, she was born in Logan, Utah, and reared in Montana. The McKay family lives in Bountiful, Utah, where Sister McKay has held many Church callings, including Relief Society president. "Bessie" is Mrs. Elizabeth Peterson McKay of Huntsville, Utah, 1969 Utah State Mother of the Year.

Grandma's Surprise Packages

FRANCES C. YOST

Grandma Benson let her tired hands rest in her lap. It was Christmas Eve and she was ready for it. She had a lovely surprise package for every one of the twenty-five members in her family, but her heart wasn't in it.

There was a hurt in her heart she just couldn't shake off, and it wasn't something she could talk over or confide in anyone. She just had to go on bravely smiling and loving all the family as she always had. Some hurts were best that way, left alone.

Grandma Benson knew the very day the hurt in her heart had started. She was just as happy as a grandmother could be, with her children and grandchildren around her, and thinking they all loved her until. . . . Well, it happened right after the Thanksgiving family get-together. Why, it was the morning after, in fact. It all happened right in the dear old room she loved.

It was a big room, with plenty of light. It was a combination living room and bedroom, with an adjoining private bath. She had all the things she loved here in the room, her books and keepsakes, and she was comfortable. If she wanted to have privacy, she could have it, and if she wanted to join the family, she was welcome. If she wanted her meals alone, one of the children would gladly bring a tray to her room. True, the furniture was getting shabby, and the rug was worn, and the curtains were mended. But it was home, and she was perfectly happy, until that morning when her son James and his wife Laura had come to her room. Grandma Benson could remember it so well, every word that had been said. . . .

"May we come in awhile and visit, Mother?"

"Why certainly, James. You know you're always welcome in my part of the house." Grandma Benson had chuckled gaily then. Now she realized she was presumptive to have said "my part of the house." None of the house was really hers; it was James and Laura's home, not hers at all. Her old home had been sold to pay expenses when Grandpa had died. And, anyway, the family had said she mustn't live alone. At that time they had appeared to mean it.

"Did you sleep well, Mother Benson?"

"Why yes, Laura. Thanks to you, keeping clean, lovely, soft sheets on my bed, I sleep like a child. I love my dear old bed."

"Mother, that's what Laura and I wanted to talk to you about. Would you mind so much living with Chris and Sarah for awhile?"

James hadn't said for how long. He hadn't said she was too much work for Laura, or that she needed a rest. Just that. Would you mind living with Chris and Sarah awhile?

It sort of took her breath, really, but she quickly moistened her lips and smiled faintly and said, "Why, James, it would be fine to stay a spell with Chris and Sarah."

She guessed she should have been moving from one child's home to another, before someone suggested it, not bother any one family too long. But she had felt so at home here with James and Laura, and they had acted as if it was all right to stay permanently.

"Well, then, if you'll pack a suitcase, I'll take you over to Sarah's place first thing after breakfast."

"Mother Benson, why don't you pack the little trunk. You know, take all the things you'll need, and your Christmas sewing and crocheting, and. . . ."

"Yes, Laura, I'll get my things right now." She turned quickly. She mustn't ever let anyone know. She must finish life bravely, serenely, no matter what happened. No matter if she were passed around among the children the rest of her days. . . .

Grandma Benson went over the last month while living here at Chris and Sarah's. They had treated her nice enough. They really had. The children had been happy to have her read to them occasionally, and she had had time to make all of her Christmas gifts. She had made cute little aprons for the smaller girls. Some were ruffled pinafores and some were appliqued with flowers or birds. The older granddaughters would receive a length of fine lace for pillowcases. They were all filling hope chests. The boys in the family would get colorful crocheted bookmarks. Boys needed to be encouraged to sit down and read, Grandma thought. The men would each receive a knitted tie, and the ladies crocheted bedroom slippers to match their favorite robes. Besides the present, Grandma had written a little personal verse for each person. It had all taken lots of time and thought. In fact, it had been good for her. When one was doing things creative, one didn't have so much time to remember hurts.

Chris and Sarah and their children had been ever so nice. She didn't have any complaints, except that Chris and Sarah were gone a great deal evenings. And Sarah usually made some excuse, almost every afternoon, to go to the library, or shopping.

Then, too, they were rather crowded. She shared a room with Janice, who was working downtown and was dating. She knew her being there was inconvenient for Janice. She never turned on the light to undress, and just felt around for her nighty and slippers in the dark.

James and Laura had come to see her quite often, but not once had they said anything like, "Do you want to come home, Mother?" She guessed she had worn out her welcome at James and Laura's completely.

Now it was the day before Christmas and they were all to spend Christmas Eve at James and Laura's. They would have the usual program, mostly the little tots singing and reciting. Then the presents would be opened and light refreshments served before each family went to its own home to await Santa's visit.

Grandma Benson had assumed the family usually came to James and Laura's because she had made her home there. Now, she realized, it was because their house was much larger. It would be different this year. Instead of her being there to greet the others when they arrived, being one of the hostesses, she now was just a guest in James and Laura's home.

Grandma Benson had a sudden impulse to pull out her lace-edged handkerchief and fill it with the tears she had held back ever so long. But she mustn't give way to grief. Not at Christmas time. Not ever! Life had been hard many times, and she wasn't going to let down when she was pushing seventy-seven. What had Grandpa Benson always said? "Keep a stiff upper lip, Susan. Things have a way of working out!"

"Are you ready to go, Grandma?" Sarah asked. Sarah always said *Grandma*. And she was her own daughter. It made her feel so old. Of course, she knew Sarah did it to set an example for her children.

"Why, yes, Sarah, I'm ready, all but my coat and scarf."

"Roger, go get Grandma's coat in the hall closet. Don't drop the scarf tucked in the sleeve." Sarah turned to the others. "The rest of you get in the car."

Then all at once they were driving up to James and Laura's. The dear old home looked so lovely, all the evergreens starlit with snowflakes. James had strung lights on the biggest pine tree, making a real outdoor Christmas tree!

The drapes were drawn, and the lighted tree in the living room was even more beautiful than when she had been there to help decorate or sit back and suggest where to hang the ornaments. And the little stockings she had made for all last year were hanging on the mantle. They had remembered to use them, even though she hadn't been there to suggest it.

The door was swinging open now, and both James and Laura were calling: "Merry Christmas, all of you!"

"Welcome home, Mother." James and Laura said together, then they looked at each other and laughed softly.

"Mother, you might as well take your scarf and coat right up."

James took her arm, and Laura took her other arm, and they were leading her up the stairs. Perhaps they didn't want her in the living room, and yet they had said, "Welcome home,

Mother." What were all the others doing following at their heels?

James swung the door to her old room open, and a silence fell on all the family, even those still at the foot of tbe stairway. Grandma Benson caught her breath and just looked. Why, a miracle had happened!

Instead of the drab old flowered wallpaper, there was a lovely soft pink on the walls. The old gray woodwork was all pink now. The dear old bed and dresser and vanity were all refinished. The overstuffed chair was reupholstered in a lovely blue. The floor was covered with wall-to-wall carpeting in a soft blue shade. At the windows hung flowered cretonne draw drapes. They had little pink and blue flowers, carrying out the color scheme of the room.

"Sarah made the drapes, Mother Benson," Laura said. "That's why she left you so much; she was sewing every minute over here. And here are the lovely hooked rugs you gave me. I cherish them as much as ever, but they just seemed to belong in this room."

"Yes, they do add a cozy touch," Grandma Benson murmured.

It was so like Laura, giving someone else what she herself cherished. Why had she doubted her unselfishness for a time? Grandma Benson had a big lump in her throat, but she must speak up. The family would think her ungrateful. What was James saying?

"All the family helped, Mother. They helped lovingly, with their hands and with their purses, and we've all enjoyed doing it. You see, we didn't wrap your presents as surprises by the tree this year; we hid them behind your own door."

"Your own door." The words were sweet to Grandma Benson. She wanted to cry, but they were tears of joy she was holding back now. Her lip quivered, but she managed to control herself and gave her biggest smile.

"You children surely did surprise me all right. And you have made me very, very happy. You're all dears, and I love you, every one. Now let's go downstairs and start our program. I want to hear the little folks' pieces, and. . . ." Grandma Benson laughed gaily as she added, "I have a few surprise packages to pass out myself."

Relief Society Magazine, December 1960, pp. 812-15. Frances C. Yost and her husband, Glenn F. Yost, reside on a wheat farm south of Bancroft, Idaho. They are the parents of four children. A free-lance writer, Sister Yost is active in Relief Society. Note: This story is fiction.

Christmas at the Desert's Edge

LORENE PEARSON

It was the day before Christmas on the dry, dust-bitten farm of Martha and Hiram Hanks. Since early morning a high wind had been sweeping across the hummocks of greasewood that caught the swirling dust about its tenacious roots.

Martha looked out the window of their drafty tar-paper shack with bitter tears in her eyes. It has been another dry, unproductive year, but drier and more unproductive than the five years just past. The garden patch had dried up so early in the spring that Martha had lost interest and let big tumbleweeds come in and crowd out what few stragglers of vegetables there were left. She looked out now at the desolate patch and knew that nothing could be more bleak and discouraging in December than a field dotted with a few stubborn tumbleweeds that had not yet been torn loose to go tumbling over the country. With this wind she had thought the last of them would have blown off. But no, they hung on like grim death, intent, it seemed, on reminding her, this day before Christmas, that her yield this year was weeds, and that meant no money at all for anything that she desired.

And all that she desired was a Christmas tree! But their

poverty would not even allow that this year. Jed Parsons went every year to the Wasatch Mountains, miles away, to bring trees in his truck.

An evergreen! What memories it brought of her own childhood in the mountains. And how she wanted little Marian to know and love those mountains she had never seen. It was the one thing that Martha had set her heart on. And now, this year, they couldn't even afford a tree.

"Hiram, I can't stand it!" she burst out. Her utterly defeated spirit that had staved off bitterness all these last miserable dry years cried out now in an uncontrolled flood of tears.

Hiram stood by her helplessly. "Come, Martha, it isn't as bad as that. Cheer up." . . .

Hiram was bewildered, hurt. His rugged, wind-burned face was set in a patient mold, and his ever-hopeful blue eyes couldn't understand this defeat of Martha's. For him there was always another year, another season that would be better than this last. But women, he concluded, could not see ahead. They lived in the present; they couldn't think in years. Tentatively he asked, "Have you no faith at all, Martha?" He hoped this might allay the revolt within her.

"Faith," she flared back at him. "Faith! I've been living on faith all these years, and absolutely nothing has ever come our way. I'm through, I tell you. I'll not live on this dry farm another year. I'm going to make some money so that my child will never again have to go without a Christmas tree."

Hiram was bewildered, upset. "You don't know what you're saying, Martha. You wouldn't leave Greasewood Flat. It's our home."

"I intend to leave, Hiram Hanks. Unless, of course," she laughed bitterly, "unless a miracle happens." . . .

That night the wind blew and buffeted and beat the little tarpaper shack on Greasewood Flat. In the darkness and tumult of the storm Martha tossed and felt the hurt of unshed tears in her dry throat. Hiram, she knew, was awake too, but he didn't toss. He lay there as though some great weight held him down. Toward morning the wind quieted, and the two of them dropped off into a fitful sleep.

It seemed as though they had just closed their eyes when Marian's shouts and the tug of her little hands woke them up to a sunlit, quiet world. "He's been here, he's been here," she ran to the bed, screaming excitedly. "Out on the porch. Come quick and look. A tree, a tree."

Martha and Hiram, stirred by the enthusiasm in the little voice, got up and, in spite of their unhappy night, felt a thrill of anticipation and curiosity. They went to the door, where already Marian had gone out before them. There, in a corner of the tiny porch, two tumbleweeds had rolled, a small one on top of a larger one. Marian had already brought out all the last year's trimmings for the tree and had draped them over the prickly, lovely branched weeds. . . .

Marian clapped her hands and danced around the little tree. . . .

Martha picked up the little girl and hugged her tight. This time the tears that ran down the mother's cheeks were not from a bitter source. In her heart Martha knew that never again would she lose faith.

Relief Society Magazine, December 1934, pp. 739-42. Note: This story is fiction.

No Christmas Tree, No Presents

MRS. BOYD LEMON

I t was still the first week in December and my Christmas shopping was finished. My fruitcake was stored in the refrigerator, the Christmas cookies were in the freezer, and the hand-dipped chocolates were ready to be boxed.

My cupboards were stocked for the holidays, and for the first time during my marriage my parents had waited to come to visit us until after the holidays. Even more important, the children and I felt that we had found "home." For the family of an Air Force sergeant in electronics, home had been many places and often changed. Here in Nevada we felt we belonged; we loved the people, the climate, and the joy of living there in the beautiful desert lands. Never had we known such contentment.

This was the first time I had been so ready for Christmas so early. With the responsibilities of eight small children I was usually never quite ready. All I had to do now was to take care of the school Christmas programs, the angel and the shepherd costumes for church, the parties and the programs, and enjoy the Christmas spirit and the miracle of love that works its special wonders at this time of year.

That Friday afternoon my husband came home and asked if I had my bags packed.

Stunned, I asked him why.

He replied, "We're leaving Monday morning for San Francisco. Our overseas flight takes off Tuesday afternoon."

My husband had received an assignment nearly eight thousand miles away, and we had been given less than three days to prepare to leave.

I stamped my foot and said, "I won't go. They can't make me go like this. And besides, even if I could get ready, the government could never get us packed and out of here by Monday morning."

My husband just looked at me, shook his head, and said, "Honey, you're on your way."

Thanks to many friends and to my parents we packed, shipped our household goods, cleaned the house, signed out, and Monday morning we were on our way. We drove all day and all night to get our car to the port for shipment and to make our flight connections in San Francisco. I cried all the way, emotionally and physically exhausted, wondering why this disruption in our lives when everything had seemed so right.

After we boarded the plane and we were in the air, I looked down at the coastline and wondered when I would see it again. I immediately dissolved into tears. I didn't want any part of this, but here I was and there didn't seem to be anything I could do about it. The thought that I could adjust had not yet occurred to me.

We crossed the international date line, which added another ten hours of darkness to our night. We lost a day, and we arrived at our destination at night. It was as dark as my spirits.

Following behind my family, I stepped out of the plane into the hot, moist tropical air of the Philippine Islands. I wondered how I would ever stand it for two years.

After clearing through customs we left the airport to go to the house that had been prepared for us. I was further dismayed by the sight of the compound fences, gates, and the security guard that patrolled our area twenty-four hours a day. In the days that followed I made a half-hearted attempt to get settled. I started with the twelve trunks and suitcases that we had carried with us.

My state of mind during the packing was clearly defined when I opened up our trunks. We found that our oldest daughter's clothes had all gone into permanent storage and she had nothing but the clothes she had traveled in.

We found valuable space had been taken up by articles that had no immediate value, and many essential items had been left behind to follow with the rest of the shipment. The final touch was the suitcase full of Christmas cookies we had hand-carried for nearly eight thousand miles.

We found our Christmas presents had been inadvertently placed in permanent storage along with our summer clothes. Our winter clothes and blankets were on their way to us, sitting practically on top of the equator.

No car, no friends, no money. Only days before Christmas, and we found out that our pay records had been lost and we wouldn't get paid before the end of January at least. We knew there would be no Christmas tree, no presents, and no festive meal with turkey and all the trimmings. After all my work and weeks of preparation, I had never felt so desolate.

But not the children. They were out exploring, excitedly living each moment of each day. They were exploring our new neighborhood, getting acquainted with the neighbors, experimenting with a new language.

One day I noticed the children walking around the house with their eyes closed, feeling their way with their hands and bumping into everything. It seemed peculiar behavior and they were all doing it, so I asked them why.

They told me that twelve-year-old Marty who lived across the street had been blind since birth. They wanted to know what it was like to be blind.

It was like being hit in the face with reality. While I was living in the past and feeling sorry for myself, my children were living in the here and now, and they were becoming involved with other people, especially Marty, a beautiful, happy child, deprived of so much by accident at birth, yet so loving and giving, and bringing joy into the lives of all who knew her.

The children found out that Marty's family had been there only a week longer than we had; the family on one side arrived the day after we did, and the family on the other side had been there only a month. We had much in common. They all had children, and they too were strangers, and lonely.

The children became completely involved with Marty, finding out how to play the games that a blind person could play. John, with his guitar, found out she liked to sing as much as our children did, and there were songfests.

The children decided to put on a Christmas program. They combined their talents, improvised costumes, and gave us the story of the first Christmas; then Marty, with the voice of an angel, sang "Silent Night."

Without a Christmas tree, presents, or a feast, it was one of our most memorable Christmases. We'll never forget it.

I'll never forget Marty and the lesson of love I learned from her, and the changes that I was able to make in my life, the willingness to accept my life and be thankful for all that I had, and the peace and joy that came into my life because of her.

At the end of the two years we were not ready to return—we stayed another six months, and enjoyed every minute to the fullest, even though Marty had long since gone out of our lives, leaving only the influence of her love and the life she lived—our most valued gift that first Christmas in that faraway land.

Deseret News, December 20, 1971, p. 1. Reprinted by permission. Mrs. Lemon and her husband, who have resided in Ogden, Utah, have eight children. Mr. Lemon was in the U.S. Air Force for twenty years, and the family has traveled extensively throughout the world.

His Brother's Keeper

ELSIE CHAMBERLAIN CARROLL

Peter saw the porter coming toward him. "The lady from the home told me to see that you got off the train okay and find the folks that are waiting for you."

Peter clutched the box containing his clean shirt and socks and the agates and pencils and other little gifts the boys had slipped into his hands and pockets when he was telling them good-bye.

Out on the station platform the porter piloted him through the crowd. "Mr. Herrington! Mr. Herrington!" he shouted.

Peter's mind went swiftly back to the fire in the shop at the home, and his rescue of Ranny, which had led to his adoption. He had not even known at the time that a newspaperman was there taking his picture as he stumbled from the building with his little crippled friend Ranny in his arms. But it came out in the papers the next morning with the story of the fire. It was that picture which had brought him this chance of parents and a real *home*, the dream of every boy in the orphanage. Mr. and Mrs. Herrington had written to Miss Younger, the matron, that the picture was so much like their own dead son that they were sending money for Peter's transportation to them immediately, before Christmas. They had made a point of that. So all day he had been traveling toward his future, his mind bewildered by the swiftness of events, his emotions so tangled he didn't know how he felt.

Presently Peter saw a tall man with a gray mustache and a plump woman in a fur coat coming toward them.

"I'm Mr. Herrington. Is this the boy?" The man stood looking down at Peter, who suddenly felt very strange and lonely.

"Yes, sir. The lady told me to help him off the train and to find you."

Mr. Herrington took a bill from his pocket and closed the porter's hand over it. Then he put his arm around Peter. The woman had reached for both his hands and was looking at him searchingly.

"See, George, the resemblance is even more striking than it was in the picture." There was a strange hoarseness in her voice. "Oh, my dear, you don't know what you are going to mean to us." She stooped and kissed Peter, first on one cheek, then on the other. Her lips were soft. She smelled sweet. Peter felt dizzy. He couldn't remember ever having been kissed before. Mr. Herrington patted him and took out his handkerchief and blew his nose.

They led him to a waiting automobile. A chauffeur in uniform opened the door, and they got in. Mrs. Herrington kept her arm about Peter. He didn't know whether he liked it or not. His mind was so confused he didn't know how he felt.

"Shouldn't we stop at the store and get him some clothes?" asked Mrs. Herrington.

"Not tonight," her husband answered, studying Peter's serious face. "He's tired. There'll be time tomorrow."

"But we have so much for tomorrow. The tree to trim, the gifts, and the party." She drew Peter closer to her. "We're glad we found you before Christmas."

He had a feeling that he should be very grateful and happy. He tried to feel that way and wondered why he couldn't.

He thought of the Christmas preparations that would be going on at the home. Old Mathews had brought the tree down from the mountain Saturday. The children would be making colored chains tomorrow. That is, all who had done their work well during the week and who had been good. He hoped Ranny had not cried after he had gone, and made Miss Younger cross, so that she wouldn't let him make chains. On Christmas morning there would be a little colored stocking or bag of candy and nuts on the tree for each one of the children from the ladies' clubs, and there would be sweaters or shoes or shirts from the home's board. Peter had hoped he would get new shoes this time. His old ones had been burned the day of the fire, and they hurt his feet now.

He tried to bring his thoughts back from such ramblings to what Mr. and Mrs. Herrington were saying.

"We have invited a lot of little boys and girls to your Christmas party," Mrs. Herrington was saying. "We want you to get acquainted and be very, very happy."

Peter wondered if any of the new boys would be like Jakie or Pudge, or if any of them could wiggle their ears like Eddie. Of course there would be no one little and lame like Ranny. He drew his sleeve across his eyes and swallowed hard.

The car turned in at a driveway bordered on both sides by snow-draped trees. The huge house, with its wide porches and great arched doors and windows, was almost as big as the main building of the home.

Inside, the rugs were so soft that they made Peter feel as if he were walking on pillows. The pictures and shining tables and great cushioned chairs seemed unreal. He tried to imagine how it was going to be to live in a place like this. But he couldn't. His mind kept thinking of what was going on at the home.

"Well, son, how do you like your new home?" Mr. Herrington asked, looking at him quizzically.

"It's—it's—grand," Peter stammered. His mouth felt dry and tasted salty. He was embarrassed to feel so shy and not to be able to respond to the great kindness of these good people who were giving him a home and the love he had never known.

A girl in a black dress and white apron and cap came to a door and said, "Dinner is served."

"In just a moment, Marie," Mrs. Herrington told her. "Peter will want to go to his room and wash and brush up a little. Come on, dear, I'll show you."

She led him up a broad stairway into a large room with a wide bed and bright drapes.

"This was Reggie's room," she said softly. There was a strange catch in her voice. "We hope you'll like it." Peter looked up at her searchingly. He knew she was wishing he were her own little boy. "Here is the bathroom. You'll find brushes and towels, everything you'll need. Come down when you are ready."

Peter stood for a little while looking about, his box still clutched in his arms. He touched the rose-colored spread. How wide the bed was! If his cot had been that wide, he could have taken Ranny into bed with him the nights he couldn't sleep, instead of just reaching over and holding his hand.

He looked at himself in the long mirror in front of him. The sight of a pale face and anxious eyes almost frightened him. His suit, which Miss Younger had sponged and mended and pressed, was all wrinkled again. His shoes were cracked where they had been burned in the fire. He studied his face, wondering how much he really looked like that other boy—the boy who was dead. This was that boy's room. He used to sleep in that bed and look into this mirror.

A shiver went over Peter. He wondered if the other boy was looking at him from somewhere up in the sky. Maybe he wouldn't like his being there in his room.

Peter, still clutching his box, hurried down the stairs.

Mrs. Herrington seemed surprised to see him so soon, but she smiled and reached out her hand. "We'll go into dinner now. You can leave your box here on this table until you go up to bed."

How different it was sitting there at this big table with only Mr. and Mrs. Herrington from sitting at the long table in the dining room at the home with boys crowded along the benches on both sides, eating soup, or liver and onions, or baked beans. The cloth was white and shiny. Rows of forks and spoons lay by his plate. Mr. and Mrs. Herrington, he knew, were trying hard to make him feel at home.

Mr. Herrington asked him if he liked to skate, and Mrs. Herrington urged him to helpings from the many dishes the white-aproned girl brought in. But Peter wasn't hungry. He wondered who was seeing that Ranny got his share of soup and pudding. He remembered that day six years ago when Ranny had been brought to the home. Peter had heard him crying and had stopped to look down into the basket which held him. The crying had stopped when Peter wiggled his fingers above the baby's face. Ranny's claw-like little hand had reached up and clutched one of Peter's fingers. From that moment Ranny had been his charge. He'd dressed and fed him. He'd taught him to stand on his twisted little legs and take his first steps. He'd held his hand in the night when Ranny's back hurt so much he couldn't sleep.

"You haven't eaten much," Mrs. Herrington said as they arose from the table. "Wouldn't you like to take some of these oranges and little cakes with you when you go up to bed?" But Peter shook his head, and they went into the big room.

"Wouldn't you like to look at some of these books?" Mr. Herrington said, going to shelves near the fireplace. "If you don't want to read, you'll find a lot of pictures."

Peter took a book Mr. Herrington handed him and sat on the edge of a huge chair. He began turning the pages. But he wasn't seeing what was before him. Soon he knew that Mr. and Mrs. Herrington were looking at him from behind the paper and magazine they were reading. He knew that they were trying to make him feel at home. He was sorry that he was disappointing them. He wished he could talk, but his throat was tight and his lips dry. He couldn't think of anything to say.

"I know you are tired, dear," Mrs. Herrington said at last. "That was a long ride, and we have so many things to do tomorrow. If you'd like to go to bed, I'll go up with you."

As they passed Mr. Herrington, he reached out and ruffled Peter's hair. "It's going to be great having you here, sonny," he said. "We'll soon get acquainted. Here, don't forget your box."

Peter picked up his precious box hurriedly. "Thanks," was all he could say. He wasn't used to men. At the home old Mathews and Terry were the only men he ever saw, and they weren't like this big friendly man in a fine black suit and white tie. Mathews and Terry wore blue jumpers and overalls like the boys. Peter understood that they had once been boys in The Home, too, boys who hadn't been lucky like him to be adopted. So they had been kept on year after year to scrub and make fires and carry garbage. He must be thankful for this good luck which had come to him. He would try harder.

"Perhaps you would like to take a bath before you go to bed." Mrs. Herrington opened the door to the tiled bathroom. Peter was sorry that he hadn't washed before dinner. But he couldn't explain about her own boy seeming to be there behind him as he looked into the long mirror.

"You'll find pajamas there in the closet. Reggie was just a little taller than you." He wished she wouldn't keep talking about the other boy.

Again that little shiver went up his back. He faltered, "Do you think he'll care if—"

"Why, bless you, no. Of course not," she tried to assure him. "He'd be happy. He always wanted a brother to share this room with him." Again he detected something in her voice which made him know how she missed the other boy. But she put her arm around him and said, "Do you mind if I kiss you goodnight, Peter?" She held him close for a moment and kissed his forehead. Peter couldn't remember that anyone else had ever kissed him. He felt a queer impulse to lay his head against the soft, sweet-smelling lace on the front of her dress and cry, and tell her about Ranny. But he fought the impulse down. Boys his age didn't cry.

"Goodnight, dear. I hope you sleep all right. And tomorrow we have a lot of wonderful things to do. Peter, it's so nice to have you here!"

As she went toward the door she said, "Our room is just across the hall, if you should want anything." Then Peter heard her going down the stairs.

For a long time he stood just where she had left him. He wondered why he wasn't happy. No boy in the home had ever fallen into such luck as this. And yet he wished he could wake up and find it all a dream. He looked toward the shining bathroom and was afraid of its whiteness and cleanness. He looked at the rose-colored bed and felt that it would be wrong to rumple its smoothness.

Finally his eyes rested upon a framed picture on the wall. Three boys were playing marbles under a huge tree. He stepped closer. The one who was shooting looked a little like Pudge, and the littlest one was about the size of Ranny.

He was still looking at the picture when he heard Mr. and

Mrs. Herrington come up to bed. They paused a moment at his door, but they did not come in.

He kept on looking at the picture. With a little effort he could imagine that the boys were Pudge and Ranny and himself playing marbles on a spring day under the oak by the workshop. His throat burned and felt tight, and the picture blurred. He hastily brushed a tear that fell onto his box, and drew his arm across his eyes.

He sat down on a little stool at the foot of the bed and opened the box. One by one he took out his farewell gifts from the boys—agates, stubby pencils, dried prunes, pennies, a black and green beetle, and a circus advertisement. He fondled each article lovingly, thinking of the words of the boys when the gifts were proffered. Finally he opened a smaller box and took out his most precious treasure. It was one of Ranny's baby teeth, wrapped carefully in a scrap of paper.

As he looked at it tears rolled unheeded down his cheeks. Maybe Ranny was lying there in the dark of the long dormitory now, his legs and back hurting and nobody to talk to him. Maybe right now he was reaching out his skinny little hand across the aisle toward Peter's empty cot.

All at once Peter knew that he could not bear it. He must get back to the home to take care of Ranny.

His first thought was to go across the hall and tell Mr. and Mrs. Herrington. But he couldn't bring himself to that. They would think he was crazy. *Anyone* would think he was out of his senses. But he couldn't help it.

A thought came. He would write a note. Then he would slip down the stairs and out the big front door. Some way he would get back to the home. Perhaps it wouldn't be too wicked to use that ten dollars left from his ticket which he'd forgotten to give Mr. Herrington.

He carefully wrapped up the tooth and put it back into the box. Then he chose the least stubby of the pencils and wrote on the back of the circus handbill Eddie had given him:

"Dear Mr. and mis harington. I am sorry i cant stay. You was awful good to want me But i have to go back and care for Rany. Hes little and lame and when his back hurts in the nite and he can't sleep hes afraid, I nede to tell him stories and hold his hand. I'm sorry about the ten dolars. Peter."

He laid the note on the rose-colored bed, took his box, and stole from the room.

A dim light burned at the head of the stairs. The great house was very quiet as he crept toward the front door. He felt frightened and lonely. He felt sorry, too, for the disappointment his going would bring to Mr. and Mrs. Herrington. Their letter had said their lives were so empty without Reggie they couldn't bear the thought of Christmas without someone to take his place. And they had offered this grand home and a place in their hearts to him, Peter, and he was running away from them. Once he turned back to the stairway, but it was only for an instant.

He had trouble slipping back the heavy bolt, and as it moved with a little grating sound, he looked behind him up the wide stairs. But nobody called or came.

Outside the snow was deep. The moon was high and bright. Peter shivered as he started down the driveway. He felt sure he could find the station, and he would wait for a train. But when he came to the highway, he wasn't sure which direction to go. He pondered a little, then resorted to a charm Eddie had taught him one time when they were sent for the cows that had broken out of the pasture at the south end of the home grounds. He closed his eyes and chanted:

"North or south, east or west,
Which of all the ways is best?
I'll whirl around and point my toe;
Where it points is the way to go."

When he opened his eyes, Peter found himself headed in the direction opposite to the one he had started to go, but he set out along the road.

The snow seemed to become deeper and deeper the farther he went, and he was soon numb with cold. Finally, he felt warmer and very sleepy. Twice he stumbled and fell. At last when he fell a third time, he decided to stay there in the soft warm snow and take a little nap; then he would go on to the station—to Ranny.

As he drifted away into unconsciousness, he thought he was

in a soft rosy bed in the dormitory, holding Ranny's hand, which wasn't skinny any more, but plump and soft and warm and smelled sweet.

°   °   °   °

When Peter opened his eyes he couldn't think where he was. Then he knew that somebody was sitting beside him, and that he was in a soft warm bed. As he stirred, the person beside him arose and stepped to a door and spoke to someone else.

Peter was beginning to remember—the home; the big house from which he had stolen away; Ranny.

Now two persons were standing by his bed. One was plump and had a lace ruffle on her dress. Mrs. Herrington. He couldn't see the other person, yet he knew someone was there.

He remembered falling in the snow. How did he get back to the big house?

"Peter," Mrs. Herrington's voice was very soft and sounded far away, "are you feeling better?"

Peter nodded, still groping in his mind.

"Peter, why didn't you tell us about Ranny? We found your note after you had gone, when I got up to make sure you were all right. Then we found you. We called up the home and found out all about how you have taken care of Ranny, how much you love him. Of course, you couldn't be happy without him when he needs you so. Didn't you know that we could love Ranny too? Well, he's here now, and he's going to stay and be your brother." She was holding Peter's hand and looking tenderly into his eyes. "And a great doctor is going to fix Ranny's back and legs so they won't hurt anymore."

She turned to that other person. "Come on, Ranny. I'll lift you up so you can see your Peter."

Peter reached for the thin little hand and whispered, "Hello, big feller."

He was very sure he must be dreaming, but he didn't pinch himself, for he wanted to go on dreaming forever.

Children's Friend, December 1948, pp. 510ff. Note: This story is fiction.

A Birthday Gift for the Lord

SPENCER W. KIMBALL

A ren't you making a cake, Mother?" asked the four-year-old as she saw her mother making preparations for the Christmas dinner.

"No, darling. Why?"

The little girl said: "We ought to have a cake today, a birthday cake. This is Jesus' birthday, and we ought to have a birthday cake for him."

The hours passed and the grandparents came in and all the family enjoyed the birthday cake for Jesus. "Out of the mouths of babes and sucklings. . . ."

In one of the stakes of Zion lives a family who also believes in a birthday for Jesus. It was on April 6, 1955; and as they gave to me a crisp fifty-dollar bill, they said, "Today is the Lord's birthday. We always give gifts to our family members on their birthdays. We should like to give a gift to the Savior. Will you place this money where it will please the Redeemer most?"

Two days later, Sister Kimball and I were on our way to Europe for a six-months' tour of all the missions. As we made hasty and extensive preparations, we kept thinking about the birthday gift entrusted to us, and then the thought came to us that perhaps in Europe we would find the most appreciative recipient.

For months we toured the missions, held meetings with the missionaries and Saints, and met many wonderful folks. There were numerous opportunities to present the gift, for the majority of the Saints over there could use extra funds. But we waited.

Toward the end of the mission tour we met a little woman in Germany. She was a widow; or was she? For she had been alone with her family of children for ten years. Whether her husband was deceased or not she did not know. A victim of World War II, he had disappeared and no word had ever come from him. It was said that he was behind the Iron Curtain. The little folks who were but children when he was taken away were now near grown, and the son was a full-time missionary among his German people.

It was nearing the time of the temple dedication at Bern, Switzerland. I said to this good woman, "Are you going to the temple dedication?" I saw the disappointment in her eyes as she said how she would like to go but how impossible it was because of lack of finances. "Here is the place for the gift" was the thought which rooted itself in my mind. I quietly checked with the mission president as to her worthiness and the appropriateness of her going to the temple; and then I gave to him half of the gift, which he assured me would pay the actual bus transportation to Bern and return.

A few weeks later we were in southern France. We had driven from Geneva south to the Riviera. The long circuitous route had taken most of the day. The bumper-to-bumper cars of the crowds of fun-lovers along the beaches delayed us so that for some twenty or thirty miles we moved slowly, inching our way to reach our destination. When we arrived, we were one hour late for our meeting in Nice.

It was a hot night. The building was filled to capacity. A woman sat at the piano, entertaining this large crowd until our arrival. For one hour she had played. I was so embarrassed for our delay and so grateful to her for what she had done to hold the group and entertain them that I inquired concerning her. Her husband, a professor, had died not long ago, and the widow was making a meager living through her musical talents. She was a rather recent convert. Her mission president and the elder assured me that she was worthy and deserving, so I left with her mission president, to be given to her, the other half of the Savior's gift.

We completed our mission tours of the ten missions and finally journeyed to Bern for the dedication service of the Swiss Temple. The prophet of the Lord, President David O. McKay, was present with three of the apostles. After the glorious dedication meetings were over, the regular temple services were conducted in the various languages. As I assisted the French Saints in their session, I was conscious of the little musician; and she literally beamed as she was enjoying the Savior's birthday gift. She had used it to pay for her transportation to the temple. Her eyes shone with a new luster; her step was lighter; she radiated joy and peace as she came through the temple with new light, new hope. And I whispered to myself, "Thank the Lord for good folks who remember the Redeemer on his birthday."

I was present again when the three German-speaking missions had their session in the temple. These faithful Saints were assembling for their first time in a holy temple of the Lord. Some of them had been in the Church for long years, and this was their first opportunity. And as these German Saints congregated, I saw the sweet mother who had received the first gift rush over to a group of missionaries, single out her handsome missionary son, and embrace him. Their eyes were glistening as they were reunited after many months of his missionary work. To meet in the temple of God, what a joy to them both! They moved about the temple together.

I whispered to the prophet their story of devotion and sacrifice and uncertainties. He was touched by their tender affection. How they wished the lost father could be restored and that they could all be sealed this day!

The light in this mother's eyes was like that of one of her German sisters of the same group who shook my hand warmly and in deep emotion said to me: "Now I can face anything. I have been through the Lord's temple, have made my covenants with my Heavenly Father, and have my own temple work done. Now I can meet any situation. Hunger, cold, uncertainties, and even war, with all its terrors, will have less fear for me now. I have the courage and fortitude to stand the severest trials."

Another year rolled round. Again it was April 6. The birthday family came again. This time it was one hundred dollars. They were pleased with the happiness their last gift brought to the recipients. Another birthday gift for the Savior upon his birthday! Two or three days passed, and the Church's general conference was in session. I had a visit from a mission president who was telling me all about his mission, its accomplishments, his missionaries and their devotion, his Saints and their faithfulness. They were Spanish-speaking folk.

In the midst of the conversation he changed the subject to say he had just received a telegram from the headquarters of his mission, advising that a humble member had just been informed by his doctors that he had cancer which could not be cured and that his time upon the earth was very limited. There was deep sympathy and real grief in the words of the mission president as he told me how anxiously this young man and his wife and several children had anticipated going to the temple at Mesa, Arizona, to unite their family for eternity but how difficult it had been to save from their very meager income because of the high cost of living. Now it would be impossible, and the father would die without having had the privilege of temple ordinances.

I asked the mission president about what it would cost to bring the family to the temple at Mesa, and he estimated that with careful planning, $100 would finance the trip. I opened my purse and asked him, "Would this $100 bring those people to the holy temple?" His eyes lighted up, and his gratitude mounted as I told him of the faithful family who every year give gifts to the Savior on his birthday.

Not long after the temple ordinances were completed, this devoted, faithful husband and father went to his reward in the joyful knowledge that his family now belong to him for eternity.

"Verily I say unto you, Insasmuch as ye have done it unto one of the least of these my brethren, ye have done it unto me." (Matthew 25:40.)

Instructor, December 1957. Spencer W. Kimball is the twelfth President of The Church of Jesus Christ of Latter-day Saints.

They Wept for Joy

WALTER F. STEVENSON

I have never seen the spirit of Christmas so profoundly manifested in such unlikely circumstances as I did on Christmas Day, 1943.

I was in a British division that was part of the American Fifth Army in Italy. Casualties had been continuous and heavy since we had landed at Salerno. By December, we were advancing slowly north of Naples—cold, very wet, very muddy, quite weary, and a little homesick. Never had the prospect of Christmas seemed so bleak and far away.

Taking advantage of a lull in the fighting, we decided to take up position on a small farm. The countryside was deserted, so we were surprised as we opened the farmhouse door to find a farmer and his wife and seven children. They invited us to join them for evening soup. When others had fled, this family had decided to stay together in their home.

God had protected them, the farmer told us. The young children, ranging from two to fourteen, had been huddled in the cellar for days. Two girls had sores on their legs, another had been hit in the back by a piece of shrapnel, and the father's arm was was injured. Most of the cattle had been killed, the barn had been burned, and the retreating Germans had taken their horses, most of their food, and some of their household items. They had no soap, no medical supplies, and very little food, but the house was sound, they were together as a family, and they didn't want to move.

With their cooperation, we set up a command post in their house. I was a medical orderly, so our commanding officer told me to do what I could for the children. The entire battery was concerned for this family, whose Christmas prospects seemed bleak indeed.

Without telling them, we collected precious bars of toilet soap, talcum powder, candy, and various odds and ends for the children and their parents. We found a small tree that had been uprooted; it was not a traditional Christmas tree, but we decorated it with silver paper, colored wrappers, and cordite bags. When we had finished, it was the best Christmas tree we had ever seen, decorated with all the love those soldiers wanted to lavish on their own families. At bedtime on Christmas Eve, we could hear the children praying for the English soldiers and their families.

When we presented our gifts to the parents early Christmas morning, they wept with joy. That Christmas dinner was something special. It was a combined operation by our command post cook and the farmer's wife. It was the first time any of us had spaghetti for Christmas and the first time the Italians had eaten English Christmas pudding. I will never forget the children's delight over such simple presents, and the hugs and kisses that brought tears to every eye. The family couldn't speak English, and most of us spoke very little Italian, but we all understood that farmer's toast: "If the spirit that is here now could be in the hearts of all men, this war would never have happened." For some of those soldiers, it was their last Christmas on earth, and for those of us who survived, it was certainly the most memorable.

_____

Ensign, December 1973, p. 14. Walter F. Stevenson, who was born in London, England, served in the British army from 1939 to 1946. He was baptized into The Church of Jesus Christ of Latter-day Saints in 1958, and has since served as a bishop and on a stake high council. He and his wife have two children.

I Cried Like a Child

JOSEPH F. SMITH

n the following letter, written from *Santa Monica, California, December 29, 1914, to one of his sons, President Joseph F. Smith relates some personal experiences which will be read with delight and pathos during the present holiday season:*

My Beloved Son: Your most refreshing and welcome letter of Christmas Eve came to my hand yesterday, and I read and reread it with pleasure mingled with grateful tears.

Your letter also took me back not only to the boyhood days of my own boys and girls, but also to those of my very own. From 1846 to 1848 and 9 I knew no Christmas, and no holiday; and, indeed, if we had a Christmas or a New Year celebration at all before 1846—or until after I was married—for the life of me, at this moment, I cannot remember it. I was teamster, herdboy, plowboy, irrigator, harvester, with scythe or cradle, wood-hauler, thresher, winnower (by the half-bushel measure or fanning-mill, later), general roustabout, and a fatherless, motherless, and almost friendless missionary, and withal, always penniless.

I say almost friendless. I had one true friend, a widow, frail, aged—but oh! so true! She was my never-to-be-forgotten and ever-to-be-loved and remembered Aunt Mercy R. Thompson.

She, like my own precious mother, never forgot me while she lived. But in their time, they had very little, and it was a continuous struggle just to live!

Then when, after these dreary experiences, my own precious cherubs began to come along, we were existing on $3 per day for each working day employed, and that in tithing products at high prices. Well, I cannot tell you how we managed to live at all, but we did! God must have helped us, for I did not steal or defraud my neighbor. I did not owe any man, woman, or child one cent, except it was my gracious Aunt Mercy who, as often as she could, slipped a favor in my way. I owed no man through all those days, and I had to work—I could not be idle.

Now again to the Christmas holidays: There [was] . . . not a dollar in cash, with which to buy one thing for Christmas. I could draw a few pounds of flour, or meat, a little molasses, or something of that kind, ahead, at the general Tithing Office and pay up at the end of the month with tithing scrip, received in payment of my labor which more than often began at 6 A.M. and ended at 11 P.M., at $3 per day in tithing pay, which was not cash.

I saw many reveling in luxuries, with means to lavish on their every want, which were far more than their needs—riding in buggies, on prancing horses, enjoying their leisure, while I— we all!—were on foot and of necessity tugging away with all our mights to keep soul and body together. Under these spiritless conditions, one day just before Christmas, I left the old home with feelings I cannot describe. I wanted to do something for my chicks. I wanted something to please them, and to mark the Christmas day from all other days—but not a cent to do it with! I walked up and down Main Street, looking into the shop windows—into Amussen's jewelry store, into every store— everywhere—and then slunk out of sight of humanity and sat down and wept like a child, until my poured-out grief relieved my aching heart; and after awhile returned home, as empty as when I left, and played with my children, grateful and happy . . . for them. . . .

After these trials, my pathway became more smooth. I began to pick up; by hard work, rigid economy, self-denial, and the love of God, I prospered. Little openings were presented, and

I improved them. . . . Oh! let God be praised. I bless you, my son, and all of you. May the Lord God bless my sons.

Joseph F. Smith,

Improvement Era, January 1919, pp. 266-67. Joseph F. Smith was the sixth president of The Church of Jesus Christ of Latter-day Saints.

Photo by Harold M. Lambert

Bag of Toys

SYLVIA RUTH GRANT

Bob's interest in the new schoolteacher had first been aroused by Denny brushing his shaggy locks of his own free will. . . .

"Oh, I know—the lad has fallen at last for Rosie Mitchell's black curls," Bob went on.

"I guess not," began Denny.

"By the way," said Bob with sudden inspiration, "Dick Crane was telling me that you kids had sure drawn a homely teacher this year."

"She is not!" exploded Denny.

"All right, all right," soothed Bob. "I was just repeating what Dick said." . . . "So that explains the phenomenon," he mused.

Bob had a sudden inspiration. "I'm driving into town today, kid," he said with elaborate unconcern. "I'll come for you after school."

"Okay," called Denny as he snatched up his books and ran out of the door.

Bob timed his arrival so that he reached the schoolhouse just as the last child was leaving. As Denny climbed into the car he said, "You sit here a minute, son. I have a message for the teacher."

Bob walked quickly toward the little one-room school-house in order that he might not lose entirely, before he reached the door, the courage that he felt beginning to slip away. Once inside he looked up to the teacher's desk and was sure even at that distance that he had never before seen eyes so deeply blue.

She smiled and stood up as Bob walked toward her.

"I am Bob Lloyd, the older brother of the lad called Denny."

"Indeed," she responded. "I'm very fond of Denny. I think he's a splendid boy."

"You will like all of us Lloyds when you get to know us. . . . Don't you think a grand way to start would be for you and me to go over to Lincoln to the dance next Saturday night?"

She hesitated a moment and then nodded. "Well, we might try it and see." . . .

Evidently Bob found the dance an excellent place in which to further acquaintance, because he persuaded Miss Moore to go again the following week.

As the Christmas season approached Mr. Lloyd found it necessary to send Bob out to Marquard on a business trip. The city was thirty miles away through a snow-filled canyon, and the trip could be made at this time of the year with sleigh and horses only.

Ordinarily Bob dreaded the trip in winter. It took a full day's travel each way and was likely to be very cold and monotonous. This time, however, he was glad to go. It would give him a chance to buy Eileen a Christmas present. The few country stores offered nothing half fine enough to suit his fancy. No, it would really be worth the trip to be able to go through a regular store, or a dozen stores if necessary, to find just the right gift.

When he told Eileen of the proposed trip, she suggested enthusiastically that he buy the presents for the school Christmas party.

Bob set out on a cold clear morning just three days before Christmas. This would give him one full day in Marquard for his business and shopping, and he would be back home again on Christmas Eve in plenty of time for the school party.

Bob had never seen the snow-covered mountains so beautiful before—the dark pines so majestic. . . .

He reached the city in good time, arranged for the care of his horses, and had his supper. Afterwards he went window shopping, trying to decide which gift would be most suitable for the loveliest girl in the world.

At last he saw it in the window of a jewelry store, a necklace of gold, antique in design, and set with sapphires. He returned to his hotel satisfied. The first thing in the morning the necklace would be in his possession.

Bob was tingling with excitement as he entered the store. The clerk held the necklace against a piece of black velvet. It was expertly wrapped in a gay holiday box and was soon safe in Bob's pocket.

In comparison with this momentous purchase, his father's business seemed very trifling, but Bob disposed of it and then turned to the task of buying presents for the school chidren. Eileen had furnished him with a list—so many books, a couple of pocket knives, bead necklaces, and dolls.

The weather observer cheerfully predicted "a real Christmas snowstorm" for the next day, so Bob arose early. . . .

By noon he had reached Martin's place, about two-thirds of the distance home. Martin was a man in his fifties who lived all alone. . . . He was surprisingly well read, and Bob had always enjoyed spending an hour or so with him when he was passing through the canyon.

He decided to stop now to rest and feed his horses and get a bite of hot lunch for himself.

Martin was glad to see him. He enjoyed occasional company but said that he needed too much elbowroom to live in town.

The horses were cared for first, and then Bob was invited to a steaming hot dinner. He would have liked to linger for a while by the warm fire, but the growing storm outside made him apprehensive. In less than an hour he arose and began drawing on his wraps.

Martin looked up in surprise. "What's the matter?" he asked. "Your horses are all right."

"Sure, I know it," replied Bob, "but I must get going."

"You don't mean to say you're going to drive on home tonight?"

"Sure I am. I've got to. It's Christmas Eve and I have all the presents for the school party."

"Well, I'm thinking the presents will have to wait until some other eve. It's drifting right now and you'll never in the world get your team through this road today."

"Then I'll have to leave my team and borrow some snow-shoes. They're depending on me and I can't disappoint them." . . .

Martin brought in the snowshoes as Bob put the toys into a flour sack and adjusted it to his back.

"Well, you've got St. Nick's bag all right," the old man said, "but you could use the sleigh that flies through the air to a lot better advantage."

"I could at that," agreed Bob. . . .

"Well, then, I guess I'm ready," said Bob, pulling on his heavy gloves. "I'll be back in a few days for the team. Thanks a lot—and merry Christmas!" . . .

The first hour Bob made good time. He was rested and warm. He knew that he had gone more than a mile and figured that if he could keep up the pace nearly this well he would reach home by dark. The Christmas party would begin at seven, and he must reach home by that time if it was at all possible.

In the next mile the going was harder. The snow kept blowing in his face. The bag on his back grew heavier.

He began to get chilled and thought enviously of Martin's cozy, warm room. Never mind—there was warmth at the end of his trip too, only another five miles away now. Five miles wasn't so far, and he would be out of the canyon for the last two of them.

He struggled on over great drifts of snow. The road was completely obliterated by now, but it didn't matter. Nothing mattered except that he must go on. . . .

Dusk was falling. If he could only get out of the canyon before dark. He must do it. He summoned every ounce of energy left and stumbled blindly on.

He was almost exhausted when he reached the mouth of the canyon. Another two miles to go and it was long since dark. He couldn't possibly make it. Bert Tanner's farm was a quarter of a mile away. He would stop there—if he could get that far—and let them take his pack on to the party.

He was almost to their gate when he heard their sleighbells. They were driving out. What if they missed him! They must not. He couldn't stand that after all he had been through.

He shouted. It was too feeble. No one could hear that and they would never see him in the falling snow. He reached the road just a minute before they swung into it and waited there. The horses stopped before Mr. Tanner realized why. He jumped out and, removing Bob's snowshoes and bag of toys, pulled the half-frozen lad into the sleigh.

When they reached the school they helped Bob into the Peabody house across the street where Eileen boarded. He urged them to leave him alone, saying that he would be all right as soon as he warmed up a little—just to tell Miss Moore that the toys had come.

He was pacing the room trying to drive some of the ache out of his limbs when Eileen hurried in, followed by Santa Claus. Bob indicated the toys and she thrust the bag into Santa's hands.

"Here," she said. "Give these out. Just use your judgment as to whom they go—and the candy and nuts are in the rear closet. I'll be back after a while."

After Santa had left she tried to cover both of Bob's cold hands with her small warm ones.

"Why—why did you do it?" she asked. "You might never have come through."

"And would it have mattered?" asked Bob.

"Yes—very much."

Half an hour later Denny left the party and came over to Peabodys' to see what had become of the teacher. She had promised to dance a Virginia reel with him. He stopped at the window and looked in. Then his mouth opened, and he stared in amazement.

There was the teacher and Bob sitting on a couch, and Bob had his arms around the teacher. She had a new gold chain around her neck and was looking all misty-eyed.

He stared at them for a few minutes and then turned slowly back to the schoolhouse. He guessed he would go and dance with Rosie Mitchell after all.

Improvement Era, December 1935, pp. 728ff. Note: This story is fiction.

Don't Involve Me

EDNA M. JONES

We'll stay home with the boys this year," Dad had announced to the boys and me on that Christmas ten years ago. "It will make a pleasant change. After all, we're with the whole family every year—it will be nice to be alone for once."

I had readily agreed; perhaps it would be easier for me to have a simple Christmas than to argue with family or friends about not drinking tea or refusing wine with Christmas dinner. But now Christmas Eve had arrived, and I wasn't so sure. The house was very quiet. Usually by now the place would be full of people, some unpacking, some working in the kitchen, and some urgently requesting complete privacy while they hastily wrapped their remaining presents.

Now all the presents were already arranged beneath the tree, and the food was already prepared. On Christmas Eve in previous years our family would dress in their warmest clothes and walk to the local parish church for midnight service. Would my husband want to take the boys tonight?

It wasn't easy being a Mormon. Only six weeks ago my husband had said, "If you know there is something you must do, go ahead and do it, but don't involve me and *don't* bring any of your new friends into this house."

I knew I had to be baptized at all costs, but I hadn't expected such indifference from my husband. Was this why he wanted a quiet Christmas, so that he wouldn't have to explain me to my relatives?

As we four settled down to our evening meal, I asked cautiously, "Anybody going to church tonight?"

"No," my husband replied. "The boys and I have decided to stay home and watch television."

It just didn't seem like Christmas. I was glad the boys had insisted on a tree and that the oldest one had taken charge of decorating it. At least the boys wouldn't find Christmas boring— the elder would be fully occupied with his soldering iron and bits of wires while the younger would be off playing soccer.

"Do we still get to open a present tonight, Mum?" asked the twelve-year-old. "Oh, go on, we always do." Eventually, with much teasing, laughing, and speculation, we each picked out one parcel. I sat on the carpet, trying to decide which one to open.

"Here," said Dad, placing a heavy parcel in my lap. It was a neat rectangular package, immaculately wrapped with a matching rosette on one corner.

By the time I had carefully eased the sticky tape off, the boys had already stripped the wrappers from their boxes and were appreciating the contents. My husband watched my every move.

Gradually, I realized it was a book with a dark blue cover. A wave of near-disbelief swept over me as I saw its title—*The Book of Mormon!* An illustrated Book of Mormon! I had heard about this edition, but the members at my little Sunday School were as new to the Church as I was and no one had a copy.

"That's marvelous! Thank you!" I exclaimed. "But how did you get it?"

"Well," he said, "I found an address in that magazine you left lying around of a bookshop in Surrey, so I took an afternoon off and drove around until I found it."

I tried to fight back the tears. "Why? I thought you . . ."
"Because I love you," he said softly. "Because I love you."

Ensign, December 1973, p. 17. Edna M. Jones was baptized in The Church of Jesus Christ of Latter-day Saints in 1962, and her youngest son, Julian, was baptized six months later. Her husband, George, became a member in 1971 and is now bishop of the Leicester England Ward.

An Old-Fashioned Romance

NORA McKAY STEVENSON

M ain Street! Main Street!" called the conductor on the snowy Christmas Eve years ago.

A group of young people, all university seniors except David Jones, who had been compelled to work instead of entering the fall quarter, started to their feet. One of them, a young man wearing a heavy fur-trimmed coat, addressed the conductor angrily:

"Say! What's the matter with you? You didn't even come in to collect our fares. I told you we wanted to get off at the theater. Now we'll have to walk back in the snow. I could report you for this."

"Oh, never mind, Art!" one of the girls interposed. "It's only a block. Besides, we ought to have been looking out for ourselves. The conductor was busy with that woman who had so many children."

"It's David's fault," laughed Margaret Haines. "He shouldn't have been telling us such interesting things about his work in the lumber camp. I hope he wants to take a girl back with him when he goes."

"If he does, it won't be you," jeered Ruth, the pretty blonde. "Can't you see he's through with frivolous women?"

"Oh, I don't know. I heard him humming 'Two Little Girls in Blue'."

They all laughed. And the girls gathered up long skirts to step down into the snow.

"I'm glad he did take us too far," said Julia White cheerily. "A walk in this lovely storm will do us good."

Julia, a serious-minded, black-eyed, pretty girl of nineteen, had not felt so happy since the evening Art had asked her to marry him. She had told Art to wait until Christmas for his answer. The girl had not been sure that she was not a little in love with David Jones until she saw the two men together.

How poorly dressed and unpolished David was in comparison. His tie did not match his suit, his hands were rough, and his finger nails broken. He was always slow about helping with coats.

Julia's mother had always said:

"When it comes to choosing between young men, always choose the finer gentleman."

"I'll do that," Julia thought, as David helped her off the car. "I'll marry Art in the spring."

Art could have helped Julia off the car far less clumsily, but he was telling the conductor that he really had no right to charge them any fare. Finally Art thrust his gloved hand deep into his pocket with angry vehemence.

"There's your money," he said, "and be quick about the change. If we miss the first of the opera I'll surely report you."

The conductor handed out the change with stiff red fingers, closed his lips firmly as if to keep back an obvious rejoinder, rang up six fares with careful accuracy, and gave the signal to go ahead. The car went on into the drifting storm.

David wanted to keep hold of Julia's hand, but she broke away and picked up a handful of snow to throw at Art as he was stepping from the car.

But Art was not in a playful mood. He brushed the snow from his beaver collar absently as he counted the money in his palm.

"Say!" Art shouted, at last catching up with the others on the curb. "We are in luck! That simple conductor gave me a five dollar gold piece instead of a nickel. I gave him a dollar and should have had seventy cents change, but I have five dollars and sixty-five cents."

"Can't you stop him?" cried Julia as they all instinctively turned to look for the car.

"What's the use, Julia?" laughed Art. "He'll make it up before he gets to the end of the line, you may be sure of that. Those chaps don't lose anything."

"That's right, Art," said one of the other young men. "Why, the other day I gave a conductor a quarter, and he went off as cool as you please. 'Where's my change?' I said. 'You gave me a nickel,' said he. And there was no one to swear that I didn't except myself, and I did not count."

"But that does not make any difference," insisted Julia. "Because one conductor was dishonest, we need not be. Art, I think it is just like stealing to keep that money." Her round chin protruded firmly, and there was a serious look in her dark eyes.

"Oh, come along!" said Art, ignoring her protest, and with an easy laugh he dropped the money into his pocket. "Just because it is Christmas you are letting sentiment run away with you. The street car company will not go without dinner tomorrow. Let's forget about it."

"All right," conceded Julia, laying her hand on Art's arm. "I guess that is all we can do."

No one noticed the look of disappointment on David's face. It was not like Julia to give in calmly without making Art promise to return the money.

"Did anyone notice the conductor's number?" David ventured.

"How stupid of me," said Art, stopping short. "I meant to report the fellow, yet I forgot to take his number! Oh well, my temper is so short-lived I most likely would have forgotten it by tomorrow anyway."

"I wasn't thinking of making a complaint," stammered David.

But already they were laughing and talking about something else and did not hear what he said. He walked soberly along, scarcely noticing the trend of the conversation, or that

Ruth Parmlee was trying to keep step at his side. David had never felt more alone at the logging camp miles and miles from any other human being. What was wrong? Had they all changed, or had he? It seemed that in the few months he had been away he had forgotten how to speak their language. Of course, he never had spent much time running around with the crowd, and he couldn't keep up a conversation of small talk.

"Julia has always been beside me before," David thought. "That is what is wrong. I shouldn't have let myself think of her as being my girl—my future wife." A tightness came in his throat that made it hard to swallow. "We are like strangers. She has changed."

The great door of the Salt Lake Theater was just ahead. In a moment the party was within its friendly shelter, stamping off the snow. . . .

"You know, I wish that conductor hadn't given us too much money," remarked Margaret. "I've heard they have to make up their accounts if they make a mistake, and maybe that poor man will have nothing left for Christmas." . . .

"It's a mistake," David reflected, as he followed the rest and slumped into an aisle seat next to Ruth. "I shouldn't have joined the party at the last minute." . . .

Just then the soft strains of the overture to *Lohengrin* filled the theater. David loved music. It spoke to him tonight of happy days in the logging camp when he had been thinking of Julia. It brought to his mind long nights in the open when he had dreamed of the girl as his wife. . . .

Once when David's eyes met Julia's he had the sensation of sitting there entirely alone with her. Then the music and voices grew in his ears, and the figures of the others again took shape on every side.

"Gosh, I'm crazy!" he muttered to himself. "I'd better get out of here." Silently David slipped from his seat and fled up the aisle.

Out in the night with the storm he felt better. . . .

"Who am I, anyway? I've got no money. I can't finish my education. I'm nobody. No wonder Julia couldn't love me. Why was I fool enough to come home for Christmas? It's a sure thing

I'm not wanted here. I might have known when her letters got so scarce that something was wrong. I'd better clear out—and stay out." . . .

As the young man neared Main Street the clanging of a street car drew his attention. Was it the same car? He started running.

The car stopped. The conductor, reaching the rear platform after taking up the fares, peered through the door, wondering why the person they had stopped for did not get on. Through the whirling snow he saw the unsmiling face of a young man. With hand on the signal strap the conductor called, "All aboard! We can't wait all night."

"Here's your change," David said in a lifeless tone. "You remember you gave a fellow with a fur collar a five dollar gold piece instead of a nickel." David held out the money to the conductor, who took it like one in a daze.

"Thank you, sir. Thank you. I haven't had time to count up," he stammered. "It would have been terrible if it had been gone. That five dollars means Christmas for my family."

"I thought it might be like that," answered David. "A fellow needs all he earns. Here's a little present for the wife," he added as an afterthought. "Tell her 'Merry Christmas' for me."

Before the conductor could protest, David had gone.

"Merry Christmas!" called the conductor, gazing in the direction David had taken. "Merry Christmas to you."

"Say, what we waitin' for?" shouted the motorman from the front platform. "We're way behind schedule now."

The conductor, looking at the money in his hand, automatically rang the bell, and the car went on into the night.

The curtain had risen for the second act when David resumed his seat in the theater.

"Oh, David, what made you miss it?" whispered Ruth.

"I think you are very foolish to let anything make you miss even a tiny bit of this wonderful opera," said Julia.

"There are some people who just can't appreciate good music," smiled Art sarcastically.

David said nothing, but their words did not hurt him. . . .

The moon and stars were shining when the opera was over. . . .

"Going to be busy tomorrow afternoon?" David said in an undertone to Julia, when he thought no one would hear.

"I don't know, why?"

"I'd like to come over," he smiled into her eyes. "What did you think of Margaret's suggestions that I take a girl back to the lumber camp?"

"I hadn't thought of it," Julia answered, "I will be busy all day tomorrow."

"Oh!" David murmured. . . .

"She's much too lovely for a fellow like me. Art can take better care of her. I want her to be happy," he thought.

When Julia reached home after the opera her parents were still up wrapping packages and filling boxes to be delivered as soon as they were up the next morning. They were the kind of people who never miss a chance to contribute to a worthy cause or to a needy person.

"There's a box to fill with jelly and things for Ellen Grow," said Mrs. White, bustling back and forth between the pantry and the kitchen. "Maybe you'll help with it, Julia. I have a few more pinfeathers to get out of this turkey."

"You mean Ellen, who used to work for us? I thought she went to Idaho," remarked Julia, absently picking out the best apples and oranges to put in the box.

"She did. It was just an accident that we found out she is back. Pa saw her husband. He's a street car conductor. The name is Murdock. Ellen and one of the babies have been sick. Poor Ellen. She always did seem more like a daughter than just a hired girl. Fill the box as full as you can."

Julia scarcely heard what her mother said. Her mind was full of her own affairs. Tomorrow Art would come to dinner. Afterward he would take her for a sleighride, and she would promise to marry him. Next Christmas she would be wrapping packages in her own home. Would Art enjoy helping her? She was filling nuts into the small corners of the box. . . .

Julia, tucked snugly beside her father in the cutter, was delivering boxes and baskets. Young George White, with the red sleigh Santa had brought, trailed the cutter at the end of a long rope. Julia loved to hear the horses' sharpshod feet on the crisp snow, the jingle of the sleighbells, and her brother's happy laughter behind them.

Ellen's was the last place they had to call.

They drew up before the uninviting little house. Scarcely a thread of smoke showed above the chimney. And when Julia opened the door, the bareness of the room momentarily drove all her cheerfulness from her. Fortunately her lack was fully made up by the pale Ellen, wrapped in a blanket beside the little stove, who exclaimed excitedly:

"Oh, my dear! my dear! There isn't a soul in the world I'd sooner see this lovely morning than my little Julia. . . . Turn around and let me look at you. Darling, you are beautiful." Ellen turned to Mr. White. "How do you keep the boys from running off with her?" She gave him no time to answer, but ran on talking rapidly until Julia wondered if she were delirious.

"We've just had a terrible time. John was out of work so long. We couldn't even buy the eggs and milk the doctor said was necessary if we wanted the children to be well. But thank goodness the children are better, and I'm nearly well. And John has a job, and last night some young man made John a present of some money. Then the company let him off early, and he came home loaded with all the good things he could carry. This is the best Christmas I've ever had. On top of it all, I'm so happy to see you." She stopped for breath, and Julia hurriedly said:

"Mother wanted to come herself, but she couldn't leave this morning. We brought a few things for the children." Mr. White was already peeling an orange for the little boy. "Mother is anxious to see you. She always was fond of you, Ellen, and is glad you are back in town. She was—." Julia stopped short, as the back door opened and a man came in carrying a bucket of coal.

"This is my husband," Ellen said quickly. "John, this is Mr. White and Julia, of whom you have heard me talk so much."

"Mr. White and I already know each other," John said, as he stepped across the floor to shake hands. "How do you do, Miss Julia." He smiled.

"Why, why—you are the conductor," Julia stammered, giving him a limp hand.

"Yes. And you are one of the young people I took past the

theater," he laughed. "It's a good thing I didn't know that I had made a mistake in the change until the young man brought the five dollars back. I could hardly have lived through such a loss. It was mighty fine of that rich chap in the fur coat to send it back so promptly. And the one who brought the money—I'll never forget him. Insisted on my taking a five as a Christmas present for my wife." John looked affectionately at Ellen. "The fellow was tall, with a very tanned face, and made me feel as if he were in some sort of trouble himself."

Julia was bewildered. She knew well that Art had not sent the money back—David! It must have been David! He had left the opera just to go out to find that conductor! And they had all said rude things to him when he returned. How could she have been so thoughtless? A lump gathered in her throat. Not another word did she hear, although Ellen and her father were both talking when she interrupted to say, "I—I think we had better go, Father. Mother will wonder where we are so long."

On the way home Mr. White looked questioningly at his daughter, but she did not speak. Neither the horses' hoofs nor the sleighbells made any impression on her thoughts. It was as if a great light had been switched on in her brain. The worry of indecision had vanished, and she saw plain as day what she wanted to do more than anything else in the world—what she had always wanted to do. She wanted to marry David. She could never marry anyone but David.

She went straight to her desk when they reached home. Quickly as possible she wrote two notes.

"Here, George, take this note to David Jones. It's important." . . .

But, even as she was writing to David, that young man stood on his aunt's porch, suitcase in hand.

"You'll know, Aunt Clara, if you don't hear from me that I'm all right. No news is good news. There comes the car." He was through the gate. "Good-bye," he called, running rapidly toward First South.

"Davie! Hey, Davie Jones!" shouted George, as he rounded the corner in time to see David getting onto the car. . . .

"What in the devil do you want? I'll miss my train," he growled.

"Here's a letter from your girl." . . .

It took the second reading to make David quite sure of the meaning of the written words.

"Dear David," he read, "I'm curious to know who's going back to the logging camp with you. Julia."

"P.S. I'll be home all the rest of the day.—J. W."

Relief Society Magazine, December 1932, pp. 711-18. Note: This story is fiction.

Christmas Dinner

AGNES JUST REID

Mary, the wife of the homesteader, bent over a bit of sewing and contemplated the coming of Christmas with much dissatisfaction. As she had thrown out the dishwater, after washing the supper dishes, she had paused for a moment to notice the great white world in all of its glistening splendor, and something within her cried out that Christmas should be different from other days. All day she had racked her brain for some suggestion; now it was growing late on Christmas Eve, and no idea had come to her.

This was their tenth year on the homestead, and, while they had never known actual want, as the children grew older she longed for things for them, things that would make their little lives happier. Now, more than anything, she would like to give them a real Christmas dinner with turkey and plum pudding. She could just picture a turkey coming out of the oven all brown and juicy, and she could almost hear the boys shouting their appreciation, for they had never even seen a turkey, much less tasted one. Some mothers might be longing for a tree on this night of nights, a tree on which would be hung fragile toys and gaily dressed dolls, but with Mary it was the material things that counted most. She had five boys, but no girls, and even if their resources had been ample, the boys would have asked for guns and spurs and saddles, things that do not go well on a Christmas tree. Besides, Mary herself had never seen a Christmas tree. She had left England when she was four years old and, since that time, civilization had been just behind her. All her life had been spent on the frontier, and most of her company had been men, but she had always found that no matter how long they had been away from home and mother, at Christmastime their thoughts would drift back to both and they would unfailingly speak of the dinner. That was what she wanted to leave with her boys, something pleasant to remember about this Christmas, something they would still recall when they had children of their own.

She had gone over her supplies. They were ample enough, but oh, so limited as to variety. In one corner of this room in which Mary sewed, a room that was living room, kitchen, bathroom, and bedroom for the boys, there was a pile of flour, sack upon sack clear to the ceiling. It was piled in a most systematic manner, leaving little tunnels all through it where the cats could pass along in search of mice, and it was elevated from the floor for the same reason. In that mountain of flour was a year's supply of bread for her ever-growing family. In the large lumber box where she kept her groceries there was rice, sugar (that must be used sparingly), dried apples, dried peaches, beans, salt, pepper, cinnamon, and nutmeg. These last two luxuries the homesteader thought they could ill afford. Then in the cellar were a few potatoes, the only thing they raised in their garden for winter use, and there was nearly always beef, from their growing herd of cattle, and always butter and milk and cream. The children were not underfed. They had ruddy complexions, bright eyes, and untiring spirits. They were in bed now, but they had not carried with them any illusions about Santa Claus.

The homesteader was visiting at the cowboys' cabin. It had been an especially lonesome winter for Mary, for he spent much of his time there. Six cowboys had found themselves out of work, and winter was coming on, so they had begged permission to occupy the tiny cabin that was on the place. They were nice enough boys, some of them forty or more, but always "boys" in the West, and Mary was glad for the homesteader to have company, but they did a good deal of smoking and swearing, so it was agreed that the children were not to go there. Sometimes she read to the children; sometimes she played games with them; but more often, she stitched away alone. She snuffed the candle for the hundredth time and got up to put more willow wood in the stove. It was turning colder. She wondered if Slim, the cowboy with the fair curly hair, was home from town yet. He had ridden in to the terminus of the railroad that morning, fifteen miles, and had expected to be back early.

Seated again at her sewing, she went over the possibilities of a different Christmas dinner, but try as she would she could not make it sound different. "Roast beef, potatoes, gravy, dried apples." Again and again she repeated the same dismal menu. She sighed heavily. Well, she would put a little cinnamon in the apples, and perhaps she could make doughnuts. There were still a few eggs that she had hoarded from the warm days of fall. Lard she never had, but there was a plentiful supply of tallow, and she used that for frying everything. Of the tallow that was left from cooking, she made every bit of soap that was used for toilet and laundry purposes and every candle that lighted their dark little cabin.

The mending done, Mary began to make a few preparations for morning. It was ten o'clock, but she would like to know that Slim was home. He was such a boy, and there were so many pitfalls in town. Every other building in the mushrooming town was a saloon. Almost in answer to her wish, she heard the snow squeaking under somebody's feet, and soon the door was thrown open by Slim himself. "Hello, Mother!" he called cheerily. "Lonesome?" "Why, hello, Slim; no, not lonesome, just a little uneasy about you. I was afraid you might be—cold." Slim was carrying a gunnysack that showed by the folds of wet and dry that it had been tied to the back of his saddle. He took out his pocket knife in true, deliberate, cowboy fashion and carefully cut the string from the sack and dumped the contents on the floor. There was a very large package and three smaller ones, quite a load for a horse to break trail with. "Mother," he said, "we thought if we'd get a turkey, maybe you'd cook Christmas dinner for a lonely bunch of punchers; and I got a little candy and nuts for the kids, too." Poor Mary was almost in tears, but before she could stammer out her thanks, Slim was gone. She opened the packages unbelievingly. What a beautiful turkey, and all dressed, and there was a sack of raisins. My, they must have cost a lot, brought all the way from California. Dear me, she could not go to bed yet; she must run down to the cellar and get some suet for the plum pudding. It must be chopped tonight, for they were going to have the best dinner in Idaho, the kind of dinner she had dreamed of but never expected to have.

Relief Society Magazine, December 1935, pp. 755-56. Agnes Just Reid was born on a homestead in the Blackfoot River Valley, Idaho. She and her husband, Robert E. Reid, who were married in 1906, are parents of five sons. Mr. Reid died in 1947. Note: This story is fiction.

It's Your Christmas, Cheryl

CAROL C. OTTESEN

It's hard for me to tell this because I was sort of immature, but I'll never forget last Christmas. See, I have this cool friend who lives up on the hill, and her family has the whole bit—big house, nice cars, clothes like crazy. But don't get me wrong—they are really nice people and are great to me. Karen's dad is in the bishopric, and they really have a perfect home life—just the kind I always thought was the ideal setup. And, by the way, she's the kind of friend who makes you feel better than you are without overdoing it.

Well, I'm over there a lot, and they invited me to come to their Christmas Eve dinner. Everything was so fantastic. I mean, we ate in the dining room with candles, crystal, china, and two forks and spoons. Her dad gave a family prayer to begin with, and then we started off with hors d'oeuvres—you know, those funny little sandwiches, without crusts, that leave you hungry. Well, everything was peaceful and relaxed even though they have six kids. When I forgot to put my napkin in my lap, Karen handed it to me when no one was looking. Everybody seemed so happy—not in an up-tight way; sometimes they were sort of down-to-earth funny.

After dinner the Millers opened their gifts to each other.

They weren't big and extravagant like I thought they'd be, just things they'd made. Greg made Steve a leather belt. Susan gave Karen some hair curlers and her mother a sample of lotion she got in the mail. Then there were stacks of notes from Terry, the littlest one, with pictures and "I love you" all over them.

But Brother Miller's gift to his wife was something else. She nearly fainted when she opened up that box and found a Persian lamb jacket! I'd never had a gift that cost over five dollars in my life. I could just imagine what it would be like when Santa Claus dropped by that night. I knew Greg was getting a stereo, and I could just see the rest of the haul. But that isn't the real reason I was so shocked. It was just the feeling there. Everything was sort of spiritual yet fun and, well, just loving, like they were really happy to be on the earth together.

When Brother Miller drove me home I felt like I didn't want to go in. He said, "Have a Merry Christmas, Cheryl. We really enjoyed having you with us." He was so warm and fatherly. I wanted to tell him how neat he was, but I ended up just saying, "Thanks, it was great!"

The door was locked, so I stood there ringing the bell and looking at the paint peeling on the house. Then there was that torn drape that the dog ripped a year ago. I just couldn't help but compare the Millers' home with our little run-down house. I heard Dad shuffling to the door in his slippers and the TV blaring in the living room. He opened the door and started shouting at me, telling me I was too late and the least I could do was stay home on Christmas Eve. It was just like he dropped a bomb on a beautiful, ideal evening. But he was half loaded and didn't really mean everything he said, I told myself. He settled down in front of the TV again, drink in hand, and mumbling about how hard up we were that Christmas.

There was nothing around that looked like Christmas but a faded wreath on the door and a cheap Christmas tree with little balls hung on with hairpins. The house was a mess and smelled of stale bacon.

Mother came to the doorway in a robe that looked like a reject from Goodwill. I could tell from her expression she had a migraine again. "Surely wish my little girl would stay home once in a while and help her mother out."

Tears were coming; I could tell from the sting in my throat. I touched my mom on the shoulder, and all I could say was "Sorry, Mom," not really meaning it.

I went to my bedroom and shut the door, kicking my little sister's shoes out of the way.

I couldn't figure how come I had to be born in my family and not some family like the Millers. I didn't have the clothes, the house, the status, the family, the spirituality. It's really hard when you're the only Church member in the family. The elders told me it would be tough and that I had a big job ahead of me of setting a good example. I tried to, but it seemed my family only thought I felt I was real big stuff for joining the Church and changing my life. But I thought at least on Christmas Dad wouldn't find fault, and Mom would feel good and cook something special.

The tears came freely by the time I'd gone through all of this with myself. I wanted to be one of the Millers and feel accepted, organized, and secure. "It just isn't fair," I thought. "It just isn't fair!" I went right to bed without saying a prayer. I just couldn't. I was so bitter I didn't think the Lord would hear me.

Christmas morning I woke late when the sun was streaming in over my bed. Christmas morning! I jumped up with that tingly Christmas feeling—half-scared you won't get what you want but knowing you just have to. I pulled my robe on and walked out into the living room. My little sister Heidi already had her new doll undressed, and Mom was digging into a big box of cherry chocolates.

"That's for you, Cheryl," she garbled with her mouth full, pointing to a box under the tree.

Dad pushed the box over to me. It was a big box with no paper but tied with varieties of leftover ribbon. Dad was real quiet and sort of looked like he was thinking of something else. I thought it would be a sweatshirt for P.E. because I needed one, but it wasn't. When I pulled the tissue away, there were the folds of the most gorgeous long dress I'd ever seen. It was one of those old-fashioned ones with a full skirt and lace and ruffles. It had to be at least a thirty-five dollar dress!

I just couldn't say anything for a minute. My breath was all sucked in.

"I just can't believe it! How fantastic!" I just kept saying that over and over while I held the dress up to me.

"Got it at Bullocks," Mom said. Dad was looking away, but I went over and sat by him. I just couldn't help throwing my arms around him and giving him a big bear hug, and I don't know how long it had been since I'd done that!

"How did you manage it, Dad? I mean, I know you can't afford it!"

He stared at the pattern on the couch and didn't say a word, but his mouth sort of tightened and twitched a little. He moved his arm quickly around my shoulder and just as quickly away. I just sat there for a while looking at the worn knees in his pants and thinking about loving and giving and what a big job I had ahead of me.

New Era, December 1972, pp. 22-23. Carol Clark Ottesen was born in Arizona and reared in Washington, D.C. A graduate of Brigham Young University with a degree in music, she has published in Church magazines and in poetry publications. She and her husband, who is in the Torrance California Stake presidency, are parents of six children. This story was based on her experiences with and observations of teenagers.

The Best Christmas Ever

HELEN H. TRUTTON

Driving alone the fifty miles from my apartment in Council City to Uncle Ben's and Aunt Sarah's farm in Willow County gave me time to reminisce about the happy holidays I had spent with them in former years. Five, to be exact, and every one filled with the spirit of true Christmas meaning.

This one would be just as glorious as all the rest. It had to be, because it would be my last one with them before Gary returned from his Church mission in Scotland, and I wanted to carry a lasting memory of an old-fashioned Christmas, free of expensive gifts, debts, and worldly frivolities that seemed so prevalent in the world. I wanted their way to be a pattern for Gary and me and our future family.

Auntie's invitation to spend the holidays with them lay beside me on the car seat, but every time I thought about it my enthusiasm took a sudden nose dive. Usually she wrote pages of bubbling, exciting plans and news, even though she would be seeing me in a few days, but this year, the sparkle just wasn't in her words. Maybe she was busier than usual, or tired, but again, she might not be well, or perhaps Uncle Ben was sick. There was nothing to do but wait.

I tried to relax a little in my driving. Traffic was very light, and I visualized Auntie at about this moment. Likely, she was hurrying about the kitchen, dressed in a crisp cotton frock with an immaculate gay apron tied around her slightly chubby waist, taking care of last-minute details. When she would spot my car coming up the driveway, she would rush out the kitchen door, still clutching whatever object she was working with at the moment, whether it be rolling pin, bread pan, or maybe a cookie cutter.

"Camille, darling, I thought you'd never get here," she would greet me with open arms. "We should see you more often." Then she would look down at her usually doughy hands and apologize. "I should be finished with all this, but I had a few last minute chores." . . .

Naturally, Miss Emily Green, Aunt Sarah's best friend, would spend Christmas with us. She always did. . . .

As I came around the last bend in the road, I caught sight of their neat white farmhouse nestled against the foothills, looking like a frosty painting on a Christmas card. . . . Quickly gathering an armload of packages from the back seat, I passed loyal old Britt without even a pat as I hurried up the steps and knocked.

There was a shuffling sound inside, and the door opened. Auntie looked at me in astonishment. "Why, I can't believe you could drive up without my seeing you. I must have really been preoccupied. Come in, Camille darling," and she hugged me closely to her as my packages tumbled to the floor.

"Aunt Sarah, are you all right?" I asked when she gave me a chance to speak."

"Of course, dear."

"And Uncle Ben?"

"Same as ever." He came forward, kissing me on the cheek. "Sarah and I were just talking about how we're going to miss you next year." He picked up my packages from the floor and loaded my arms again. "We're mighty happy for you, though."

"He's a lucky one." Auntie squeezed my hand. "Here, let me help you with those packages. I hope you haven't spent money on us."

"Not much. Most of them I made. You taught me that," I said as we walked into the living room and placed the gifts under the tree. And then I noticed Emily Green was missing.

"Where's Emily?"

Aunt Sarah turned away, but not before I saw the hurt look in her eyes.

"She isn't spending Christmas with us this year."

"Why?" I asked, astonished. "Is she ill?"

"No. Well, she's just not spending Christmas with us, that's all. Now, if you'll excuse me, dear, I'll finish up in the kitchen," and she hurried out of the room.

"Why?" I repeated, turning to Uncle Ben. "Emily is always here. She doesn't have any near relatives."

"I know, but things are different this year," he said, looking to make sure Aunt Sarah was out of hearing before he sat down beside me. "You see, they had a misunderstanding. Emily likely wouldn't come even if Sarah asked her."

"They've been friends since they were children. Besides, it just isn't like Auntie to hold a grudge."

"Sarah is miserable," Uncle Ben sighed.

"Do you mind telling me about it?"

He ran his hand through his thick gray hair before speaking. "It's ridiculous. Last fall, just before the county fair—" he hesitated a moment "—Emily raises dahlias, you know."

"Yes, I know."

"She had a rare beauty. Sarah went up to see it a few days before the fair, and, well, Britt tagged along. That's not unusual," he looked quickly at me. "He often does."

"Go on."

"I don't know what got into that dog. He saw a mole digging, of all places, right by that prize dahlia, and before Sarah or Emily could do anything, he dug the plant up, trying to get the blamed rodent. Emily was furious."

"I suppose she would be disappointed, but she must have known it wasn't Auntie's fault."

"She should have. Sarah apologized and offered to pay for it. She even offered to give Emily her best dahlia." Uncle shook his head sadly. "Sarah didn't even enter her dahlias in the fair out of respect for Emily's bad luck."

"If Auntie apologized, even offered restitution, what more could she have done?"

"I don't know, Camille. Sarah thinks it's up to Emily to speak up now."

"I see."

"I hoped Sarah would try again, but she has not."

"I'm sorry, Uncle Ben."

Auntie came back into the room and sat down opposite us. "Is Gary still happy on his mission?" she asked.

"Yes, very," I answered, wondering if she had heard our conversation and come in to change the subject. "He's a wonderful missionary."

"I'm sure of that," she smiled. Then, leaning back in her chair, she looked mutely out the window for several minutes before speaking again. "It's getting late. I'll fix something to eat."

"Let me help you." I followed her to the kitchen. "Do we go to the usual places tonight?"

"Mostly. The Simpsons had a bit of bad luck this year, so we'll include them." She handed me a pitcher of milk. "And there's a new family moved into our community."

"Oh! Aunt Sarah," I asked, after a silence, "couldn't I talk to Emily?"

She glanced up quickly. "Ben told you?"

"Yes."

"No, dear. It wouldn't help," she said, opening the refrigerator and reaching for the eggs. "It's up to Emily now."

"I could try."

"Emily doesn't want my friendship. Would you like to set the table?"

"Of course."

In a few minutes we sat down to a platter of scrambled eggs, warm bread, raspberry jam, a pitcher of milk, and cookies. After Uncle blessed the food, Aunt Sarah smiled across the table to me.

"You've been like a daughter to us. We'll be lost without you." . . .

Within a short time the car was loaded and we were on our

way. These, I thought, are the things I'm going to miss, living in a strange city—driving along a country road . . . greeting old and dear friends, like the Kennedys, Emily, Sister Marsh, and others, riding through the countryside in a car filled with the spicy fragrance of new-made cookies and bread. Most of all, though, I would miss the two wonderful people sitting next to me. Only Emily should be here with us, too, like old times.

We were passing her house now. It seemed that Uncle Ben slowed down a little, but Auntie only glanced momentarily in that direction and then looked the other way.

Our first stop was at Sister Marsh's home. . . .

Half an hour later, we left Sister Marsh and drove to the Kennedys. It was my favorite stop. Just watching six excited, happy faces converging upon us and listening to their gay chatter was reward enough for anyone. . . .

After leaving the grateful Kennedys, we stopped at Brother Barnes'. He was delighted to spend Christmas Day with us. Next we went to the Carsons, the Simpsons, and the new people named Sanders. Then the Wilsons, an elderly couple, and, finally, we were on our way home.

We passed the Kennedys' again, and it was in darkness, and once again, we came to Emily's. From the road, I could see a small light flickering through the window. Uncle Ben started past just as Aunt Sarah called, "Stop, Ben, a moment."

Uncle Ben brought the car to a stop and waited. No one said anything for several seconds. Finally Auntie spoke. "I can't have peace in my heart and be at odds with anyone." She looked at Uncle Ben and then off into the distance. "It is the birthday of Jesus. He was the Prince of Peace. I'll ask Emily to spend Christmas with us."

Uncle slipped his arm around her waist and smiled down proudly at her. "I have the best wife in the world."

"I always thought I was the lucky one." She patted his arm. "I won't be long, Ben. Want to come along, Camille?"

We walked quickly up to the door, and Aunt Sarah knocked. No one answered, so she knocked again a little louder. Then we saw Emily coming to the door.

"Hello, Emily," Auntie greeted her.

"Hello," she answered.

"Emily," Aunt Sarah smiled at her. "I want us to be friends again. We want you to spend Christmas with us. Please forgive me for being so stubborn in not asking you earlier. I wanted to."

Emily looked away a moment, then her eyes filled with tears. "Your heart is so big, Sarah. I'm the one who should be apologizing to you. I've been too stubborn to admit I was wrong." She was crying softly now, and Auntie put her arm around her and repeated, "You will spend Christmas with us?"

"If you want me, Sarah. Come in." She stood aside for us to enter and, for the first time, noticed me standing back of Auntie. "It's good to see you, Camille."

To say the least, we were a happy foursome on our way home. Emily and Auntie chatted continuously, with Uncle Ben and me joining in every opportunity we found an opening. That wasn't often.

Soon we were back at the farm in the living room, taking off our wraps and settling in our usual places, just as we had the past five years. Uncle Ben strolled over to the fireplace and poked at the fire before picking up the Bible from the table and sitting down in his usual favorite chair. As always, he was going to read the story of the first Christmas from the second chapter of Luke.

Leaning back contentedly in my chair, I watched the flickering blue and yellow flames dart crazily from log to log in the fire as I silently mused: if you toss one pebble in a pond, the waves spread and reach out. Peace was like that, too. If only people of all nations could feel the deep need to have peace in their hearts for all mankind, if they were willing to go the second mile, as Auntie was tonight, they would be following the teaching of the one whose birthday we were commemorating.

Reaching out, I took Auntie's and Emily's hands in mine. "You know, this is the best Christmas ever."

"It sure is," Emily smiled through tears.

Relief Society Magazine, December 1962, pp. 890-96. Helen H. Trutton, a native of Idaho, has had more than fifty stories and poems published. Active in the auxiliaries and genealogy work in the Church, she resides with her husband in Walla, Walla, Washington. Note: This story is fiction.

Say It Louder, Louder

IVALOU LAWRENCE

ure white snow spread like a glisten-
ing blanket over the hills and valleys. Large drifts lay against the
house and the barn like sleeping giants. The trees in the orchard
barely showed their tips above the snow. It was Christmas.

It was always a joyous occasion in our four-room home at
this season of the year. There were five children in our family in
this special year of 1915. I was the middle child and was six years
of age. How we loved the pine fragrance coming from Mother's
and Dad's bedroom, which also served as a living room. The
Christmas tree had been cut from the hillside on our farm. It was
especially beautiful to us because we had made the decorations
ourselves. We were looking forward to Christmas morning when
we would receive homemade gifts of clothes and toys. We were
a happy family.

To make it even more enjoyable, a pre-Christmas party was
held each year in the old rock church at Mink Creek, Idaho.
There was always a program and a dance for the children. Santa
would come and pass out horehound and licorice candy. Sometimes we would each receive a popcorn ball. What fun we all
had! Now the morning had come when we would see Santa
again.

In our hot-brick warmed beds, we waited for Mother's call. Then we came hurrying down the stairs, from the two ice-cold bedrooms, into the cozy, warm kitchen. Mother stirred the fire and put more wood into the stove. We washed in the old tin basin and dressed in our Sunday clothes. The older children helped the younger children.

Dad hitched Dick and Brig, the gray team, to the sleigh. He put hay in the bottom of it for us to sit on. Quilts were brought to put over the hay. Other quilts were placed over us so we were packed between them like meat in a sandwich. Dad took his place as driver. I can still visualize him standing at the front of the sleigh, with warm mittens on his hands holding the reins. He wore a visor cap with ear flaps, a heavy coat, and buckle over-shoes with his pant legs tucked inside them. It was a beautiful day. The air was crisp and clear. I could see Father's breath as it condensed and floated away in little wisps. He cracked the reins, and we were off. The crunching of the snow and the ringing of the sleigh bells made a lovely sound as we snuggled together for warmth.

The huge tree at the church was decorated with paper chains and strings of popcorn. A big star was tied to the very tip-top. We gazed in wonder at the many small gifts that were fastened among the decorations. They were store-bought too! This was something we didn't often see in those days.

The program consisted of Christmas songs and a tableau of the manger scene, which was a thrilling sight to us. I gave a recitation—and I did it loudly, too. I almost shouted it because my father had helped coach me. He said, "Say it louder, louder! There is no use getting up there if people can't hear you." I suppose people heard me, because I was on many programs after that time. I suppose, also, that here was the beginning of a problem that I have had to fight most of my life. I talk too loudly. That day friends and neighbors complimented me on how well I did, and I was happy.

When the program was finished the most marvelous thing happened. Santa Claus came jingling his bells and "ho-ho-ho-ing." The children all sat spellbound in anticipation of what was to come. I saw Santa take one of those gifts from the tree and throw it to a tiny girl. He threw many of them to the smaller children. Then I heard him say, "Here is one for Ivalou!" I gasped as my daddy caught and handed to me the most beautiful coin purse I had ever seen. It was brown leather with a heavenly white kitten painted on it.

The Christmas spirit that radiated that day amongst relatives and friends sank deeply into my heart and made this a Christmas I will never forget.

Deseret News, December 18, 1972, p. 1. Reprinted by permission. Ivalou K. Lawrence, a former schoolteacher and native of Mink Creek, Idaho, has traveled extensively with her husband, a civil engineer, and has spent Christmas in many places, including Thailand. The Lawrences have two children and reside in Salt Lake City.

Photo by Harold M. Lambert

A Star's Slim Light

ALICE MORREY BAILEY

Luke McKean knew the situation was of his own making, and a part of the large folly which had dogged him intermittently for the fourteen years he had been a foreign correspondent for *Life*—going home for Christmas. Well, here he was right in the middle of Christmas tree land, with the Christmas landscape covered by the snow which bogged down his rent-a-car and shut him off in the wilds of the mountains between Wyoming and Utah. He had been warned in Denver, where his plane was grounded, and again in Cheyenne, but he had pushed stubbornly on; his urge to get to Salt Lake City his only companion. He had come too near his goal to give up now, even though it was far into the afternoon toward Christmas Eve.

He got out of the car again, scooped snow, pulled sagebrush, and tore at the rocks with his heels. He tried again and again, rocking the car, and finally in desperation gunning it until the wheels spun, but it was no use; he was hopelessly stuck. He could run out of gas and then not be able to heat the car. He could run the battery down by playing the radio for storm warnings.

It was irony to come so near and not make it; it was folly to try, because there was no home to go to for Christmas. He could go only to the little house where he used to live with all his hope for the future—little David and the promise of many more like him, and Mary, his wife who had waited out the war there, both of them cut off in one blinding second of slippery ice, crashing metal, and splintering glass, with himself the only anguished survivor. He could go back only to the memories he had run from these fourteen years, the bitterness of all that was lost, not to the warmth of holding Mary in his arms, the joy of companionship with a small boy.

It was silly. What could he do when he got there? Walk up to a strange house where he used to live and knock? Then what? Suppose it were vacant or torn down? If someone came to the door, what could he say? They might think him crazy, even call the police. For a grown man who could surely consider himself a cosmopolite after his wanderings about the globe, a newsman stripped of illusions, to be the victim of his own emotions was outlandish, but there it was. Too well he knew that the craving would return again and again in some strange land across the world. This was the only way to, at last, lay an old ghost.

If he didn't make it, so what? It was not his birthplace; in reality not even his home. Mary had come to Kearns, Utah, with him during his soldiering days, and he had hopped off there, leaving her to wait in Salt Lake City while he covered the European arena with his camera after a promotion through *Stars and Stripes*, the serviceman's newspaper. When he got back, Mary was sold on the place.

"I like the people and the climate, and it's the place where I want to rear our chidren," she had said.

"You going to be a Mormon?" Luke had teased, but she had answered him soberly.

"I think I am, and I want David to be one, too."

One place was as good as another to Luke, who had no family ties—no religious ones, either. He was a photographer, and surely the vicinity offered an endless parade of subjects. Luke had thought seriously of opening a studio. The loss of his wife and son in such a cruelly short time had catapulted him into his present occupation.

His present assignment was "Native Son Rediscovers

America," but it had not been like coming back to the America of Washington and Lincoln, the California Gold Rush, the covered wagon and sagebrush, or even of the war years. It was like coming to a new land, even a new planet—the coming true of the science fiction of his boyhood. . . . He left Scotland by jet in the dawn, had lunch comfortably in New York. He could have seen the sun set in Denver, slept in San Francisco.

He had gone through his assignment in excitement and wide-eyed wonder. He had been awed by dams and dynamos, automation and communications, electronics and nucleonics. He had been amused by gadgets, amazed by the surrealistic nightmare of freeways in downtown Los Angeles where four layers of traffic sped in diverse directions. He had used striped toothpaste and taken helicabs from hotel to airport, used vending machines that changed folding money, and tuned his TV by push button from across his hotel rooms.

But what about the people? Luke was still not satisfied. He had talked to literally hundreds of them, but only superficially, in spite of his penetrating newsman's questions. You can't talk to people on the run, and that was what Americans were—even as he had been throughout the last three months. Whole families were driven by schedules, from the tiniest tot with her dancing classes to the busy executive with split-second appointments. The clock was the most important instrument in the nation. Luke had seen the physical and the intellectual America, but he hadn't yet been fully exposed to its spirit and its heart.

Were the critics right? Was it true that America was materialistic, in pursuit of money and possessions instead of values, fun instead of joy? What were the young Americans really like?

Luke had a personal stake in his quest. If his son had lived, what would he be like? Luke was almost afraid to know.

How long he pondered he did not know, but, all at once, bobbing up from behind rises, disappearing in the low places, a car was coming toward him through the storm, its lights on, although it was not yet dark. Luke got out and stood beside the road. He thought amusedly that if he were a modern wise man in pursuit of a nebulous dream, here, at least, was a modern star.

The youth who unfolded himself from the Volkswagen was as tall as Luke himself, and Luke was a tall man.

"You stuck, sir? Can I give you a hand?"

"You surely can," said Luke gratefully.

They worked for half an hour to get Luke's car out, but it was no use. The young man applied himself as if he were personally involved and did not give up until Luke finally said: "I'd better go into town, if you'll give me a ride, and have a tow car out tomorrow. My name's Luke McKean."

"And I'm Peter Brent," the young man responded, quickly stripping off a wet glove to shake hands.

Once inside the car Luke had time to study the youth in the faint light from the dashboard in the growing dark, to watch his skillful manipulations of the car through the storm on the slippery road. He had features as classic as those on the head of a coin, a bright, intelligent, open countenance. Luke had to fight down a growing feeling of kinship with the boy, to keep objective, because here was his probable last chance before a new assignment, a captive specimen at his disposal for two hours.

"What brings you out on a night like this?" he began.

"My girl. She's a college student at Brigham Young University, lives in Evanston. I took her home for the holidays. What brings you out, sir?"

"Something as elusive as the Holy Grail," Luke answered evasively. He had no intention of being the interviewee, or of tipping his hand, and it wasn't his habit to lie. "I have been trying to figure out how old you are."

"Nineteen."

"I would have guessed a year or two older," Luke said. Nineteen! Just the age David would have been. If he had lived what would he have been doing now? It was a little shock to realize he had always thought of David as a small boy.

"What do you do—work, go to school?" he asked, trying to hide his growing eagerness.

"I'm in my second year of college."

"Aren't you a little young for that?"

"Maybe. I was lucky. One of the few who went into college instead of my last year of high school. It's an experiment. Gave me a lift on my major."

"Which is?"

"Science, of course," he said, as if it were all one word of a foregone conclusion.

"I hear the graduates in scientific fields can go to work at top salary when they graduate."

"That's a point," admitted the boy. Probably the most important point, Luke thought, if the critics were right.

"You'll be out of college by the time you're twenty-one."

"Not exactly," said Peter. "I have a call to go on a mission for my church. I'm leaving as soon as school's out in June—be gone two years."

"Then you're a Mormon. Don't you resent having your school broken into? Is it mandatory? Don't you dare disobey? Would it not be better to wait until you are through college?" Luke had met briefly a few missionaries from the Latter-day Saint Church in his travels; he had attended a soul-stirring concert of the Tabernacle Choir when it toured Europe, and he was conversant with the tenets from his brief stay after the war. He had never met the question head-on, remembering Mary's early desire, nor had he cast it from his mind.

"You have the wrong slant, Mister," Peter said, a little nettled. "I want to go. I've long planned on it. My only worry was that I might not be called. It just so happens it fits in with my plans for school—my lower division behind me. When I get back I want to go all out and not stop until I get my Ph.D."

"Well, then, you are a young man with a direction," Luke said, and added as a goad, "if it is the right direction. How do you know it is?"

Questioning was Luke's business; he was past master at separating information from individuals, and he had more than a small smattering of science, philosophy, and comparative religion. He questioned Peter through the skies and around the globe, parrying him at the edge of sword-sharp wit, and backing him into verbal corners. He had the young man at the rapier point of logic many times, but always Peter acquitted himself, sometimes sending the weapon flying from Luke's hand. He didn't always have the proof, but he knew the basic principles, and he warmed to the fight, thought through each question with deliberation and logic.

Peter's God was as big as the universe, with creation un-
limited, love unbounded, yet he had certain definite characteris-
tics, and Peter knew he lived with a passion Luke thought had
died with the last apostle. There were conviction and authority
in his voice. "We have the answer to all the troubles in the
world," Peter said. Luke frankly envied him.

On other matters he was just as sure. No, Russia would never
conquer America. No other nation ever would, so long as it was
a Christian nation and held fast to its principles of freedom.
It was a chosen land, a promised land, even the Garden of Eden.
Science was wonderful, as far as it went. Scientists were on the
way, faster now than ever, and when they learned everything
there was to know they would know the vast laws of God. Luke
could not disagree.

By the time they came to Parley's Canyon, with the city
spread before them like a lap of multicolored jewels from the
mountains to the lake, Luke was satisfied about Peter, but there
were still some riddles. Of what was he a product?

"You'd better drop me off at a convenient hotel," he said,
dreading the thought of another Christmas Day in a hotel.

"Not a chance," said Peter. "My family would never forgive
me—a stranger alone on Christmas."

They drove to a large, comfortable-looking home, not in the
most deluxe district, nor yet in the less-than-average, and Luke
told himself this was good; it would further his research. In truth,
he had to know more about Peter, not lose touch with him. If
David had lived would he think as Peter thought, live as Peter
lived?

The house was blazing light from every window in true, out-
going Christmas spirit, and Luke was aware of a sudden little
feeling of dread. Could it be jealousy? They had talked of everything under the sun except Peter's parents. Somehow Luke had
avoided the subject. Was it because he was identifying this boy
with David, and himself as Peter's father? At least, at the door,
there was a brief reprieve.

"I've brought home one of the wise men," the boy told the
flushed, motherly woman who came to the door. "Aunt Mel—
Uncle Dick, is it all right if Mr. McKean spends Christmas with
us?"

"More like one of the stupid men," amended Luke, not giving them a chance to say no. "Are you sure I'm not putting you out—a stranger on a holiday?"

"You won't be a stranger long, not with this bunch. Peter, put Mr. McKean in the little bedroom, and then come to the table, both of you. I haven't time for introductions. The gravy's boiling over."

Luke was overwhelmed. If this was the real heart of America, it was a pulsing one—a big family, pretty girls, another grown boy putting chairs around the dining table, steaming food being brought from the kitchen. It was a kaleidoscope of sparkle and movement—a lighted Christmas tree which touched the ceiling, flashing with light and color, the floor underneath heaped with gaily wrapped packages. Oh, this was the kind of Christmas of which Luke had dreamed! By the time they were all seated, he had slipped into the family so easily he knew all of them—Aunt Mel, Uncle Dick, Peter's cousins, Sue and Virginia and Mary Ellen, and Richard, who was Peter's age, also going on a mission. Where exactly did Peter fit into the household?

"Where's Mother?" Peter said.

"She went to give her 'Star' lecture," Aunt Mel answered. "By the way, she was worried about you."

"Don't kid me," said Peter callously. "She never worried about me a minute in her life."

Well, here it is, thought Luke. No family loyalty—perhaps divorce.

"Good reason," Aunt Mel said complacently. "You never gave her cause."

"Speaking of angels," someone said. The door opened and a shower of parcels dropped from the hands of the smartly dressed, slim woman at the door. Peter jumped to help her.

There was no doubt it was his mother—the same feminine counterpart of his classic features, the same bright, intelligent face.

"You're just in time, Jennifer. Virginia, get Aunt Jen's plate from the oven."

It was some time later, after all the introductions and explanations had been made, the dishes done, and the children gone—Richard to see his girl, Sue and Peter caroling, and the other two subbing-for-Santa, that Luke was able to make his way to Jennifer's side before the fireplace.

"I'm impressed with your son. Is he a special dispensation?"

"No, run of the mill. It's hard to tell him and his friends apart at this age. They dress the same, have the same goals, talk the same."

"Really?" marveled Luke. "I have been wondering about his father." Luke couldn't refrain from the question.

"His father was killed in the war. Peter never knew him, but he is surprisingly like him. Mel and Dick took me in when I was so broken up, and somehow we just stayed. It has been a marvelous arrangement—Peter got the normal background of a large family life, and I was able to be part father and mother to him. Now, what about you? What brings you to Salt Lake City?"

Luke told her everything without reserve, because she was the kind of listening, perceiving woman to whom a man could talk.

"And the house?" she queried. "When are you going up to knock on that door?"

Luke pondered. Where had the desire gone?

"I know now what it was," he said at last. "And it wasn't so silly after all. I wanted to know what David would be like if he grew up as his mother wanted him to grow. I found out, talking to your son. That was the door. I have already found it. I have already knocked!"

He looked into Jennifer's eyes, and the door swung wide and wider.

Relief Society Magazine, December 1966, pp. 898-903. A prolific and successful free-lance writer, Alice Morrey Bailey has won numerous prizes for her stories and poems. Born in Joseph, Utah, she now resides in Salt Lake City. She has also been a teacher of sculpture. Note: This story is fiction.

How the Pioneers Celebrated Christmas

E. CECIL McGAVIN

hristmas always had a strong appeal to the pioneers and was observed by them no matter what their conditions were.

During the autumn of 1847, the harvest was so meager in Salt Lake Valley that no special Thanksgiving service was held, yet the pioneers did not fail to remember Christmas. Though food supplies were scarce, and their reasons for merriment were limited, Lorenzo D. Young wrote of that first Christmas the pioneers spent in the Salt Lake Valley:

> I gave a Christmas dinner. Father John Smith, Brother John Young, Brother Pierce, and their wives, and also Brother Jedediah M. Grant, Sister Snow and Harriet and Martha took dinner with us. After dinner Father Smith blessed our little Lorenzo. The occasion was a most pleasant one and the day was spent in social chat, singing, etc. A prayer was offered up by Brother Grant. Brother Brigham and his quorum were remembered in particular. My house was dedicated to the Lord.

During the Christmastide in 1847, it was written in the *Journal History* concerning the Church members in Iowa:

> Friday, December 24. President Young and party proceeded to Miller's Hollow [now Council Bluffs, Iowa] where the brethren had built a log house, forty by sixty feet, capable of seating about one thousand persons. The house was dedicated by Elder Orson Pratt as a house of prayer and thanksgiving.

The congregation was addressed by Elders Wilford Woodruff and Orson Pratt, and in the afternoon by Elders Amasa M. Lyman, Geo. A. Smith, and President Young. Elder Wm. I. Appleby preached during the evening service.

Saturday, December 25. The Council went to the Log Tabernacle in Miller's Hollow, Iowa, and attended conference meeting. The congregation voted that the High Council on the east side of the Missouri River should have all municipal power given to them by the people, and that the Bishop's courts should have authority as civil magistrates among the people, until the laws of Iowa were extended over the Saints.

December 26. Elder Orson Pratt met with the Saints in St. Louis, Mo., when they donated $705.84 to assist the Presidency of the Church to remove to Great Salt Lake Valley.

On Christmas Day, 1849, a gay party was held in President Brigham Young's home. One hundred and fifty persons had been invited for the occasion. "The tables were twice filled by the company," we read, "and all were feasted with the good things of the valley. When the tables were removed, dancing commenced, which was continued with energy and without interruption, except for supper, till a late hour."

At the same time in Kanesville, Iowa, a similar social was held. "In the evening we had a little sociable dance," we read, "the party being composed mostly of Philadelphians."

On December 25, 1851, Captain Pitt's band, consisting of twenty-six members, promenaded the streets of Salt Lake City "and played before the houses of the First Presidency, the Twelve Apostles and others, while riding on horseback."

The *Journal History* contains a complete and interesting account of the celebration at Christmastime in 1851, from which we quote:

Christmas Day. Fine weather prevailed in Great Salt Lake City. All the hands engaged on the public works attended a picnic party in the Carpenter's Shop on the Temple Block which was cleared and decorated for the occasion. Several hundred persons attended and enjoyed themselves in both dance and song. President Brigham Young was also present. The enjoyments were varied with songs and addresses. The brethren of the band serenaded the inhabitants of the City from midnight till daylight which was quite a treat.

Elder George D. Watt gives the following account of these Christmas festivities:

Early on Christmas morning, Thursday, December 25, several companies of serenaders, with brass instruments made the sleeping mountains echo with the sound of rejoicing. Our attention was drawn more particularly to the Governor's mansion, in the front of which was drawn up in military order a troop of horsemen. This was the brass band, giving his Excellency a good wish in sweet strains.

At ten o'clock a.m., the committee of management was in respectful waiting to receive those who were invited to the party. The carpenter's hall, one hundred feet long and thirty-two feet wide, is admirably adapted for a mammoth party, which was comfortable, and suitably decorated for the occasion. Now the merry workmen, with their happy wives, and smiling daughters, clad in genteel apparel, came pouring in from every quarter, loaded with an abundance of luxuries of every description which were deposited in an adjoining hall, called the machine room, which is forty feet square, in which also was situated the ladies' dressing room.

At 11 o'clock the house was called to order, and a suitable prayer and thanksgiving was offered up to the Donor of all good by Bishop N.H. Felt. The band then struck up a merry tune, and his Excellency, Governor Young, and Hon. H. C. Kimball and other distinguished personages led off the first dance.

The excellent order, the quick succession of dances do great honor to the managers. We counted from ninety-six persons to one hundred forty-four persons upon the floor at once. These were set in order to the same time that we have seen four cotillions in other parties. There was no confusion, no dissatisfied looks, no complaining, but the day passed in peace and happy merriment, with thanksgiving to the Father of all our mercies. . . .

The atmosphere of our hall was not polluted with tobacco fumes, or the stench of the drunkard's breath. No! We breathed the pure mountain air, drank of the mountain stream, and ate of the produce of the mountains' valleys, we thought on the gloomy past, and the glorious present, and perspective future, every heart beat high with gratitude and gladness, and every countenance was lit up with the bright fire of enduring friendship.

About seven p.m. a few songs were sung by sundry individuals; one in particular called up feelings not strange to us was sung by Phinehas H. Young, entitled "Farewell to Nauvoo." This song gave the company ample opportunity of comparing the present with the past.

Governor Young arose to address the meeting, and congratulated the assembly on their present situation and blessings as a people.

On Friday evening, December 26, the "public hands" again met in the Carpenters' Shop where "dancing was kept up with great spirit until midnight when all separated highly delighted with their Christmas festivities. In the course of the evening Willard Richards spoke of the difference between this evening and the 27th of June, 1844, when the tragedy at Carthage, Illinois, took place."

Elder George D. Watt gives the following account of this festival:

The seats in the Carpenters' Hall were filled by the not to be surpassed fair daughters of Zion, and the brave hearted sons of God.

The company was called to order, and prayer was offered up by A. H. Raleigh. The dancing was conducted as on the previous day, and the same good order, joy and hilarity was manifested.

After the Hall was illuminated, the company was treated to a feast in the shape of vocal and instrumental music by Mr. John Kay, his lady and two daughters, the one performed well on the Guitar, and the other on the Tambourine, at the same time accompanying their instruments with their voices, this with the sweet voice of Mrs. Kay, and the deep bass of Mr. Kay produced a species of harmony highly delightful to the ear. The performance was much applauded. Brother Kay sang the Seer, in his usual pathos and sweetness, which drew from President Richards, a few touching remarks. Elder George A. Smith also addressed the meeting for a short time, after which the dance was resumed, and continued until 10 o'clock p.m. A vote of thanks was moved for the managers, which was responded to by 500 voices. After the benediction from Father Cahoon, the assembly retired, much gratified with their Christmas festival, which was the best they had ever witnessed.

In some of the communities of the Saints there were not enough food supplies to furnish the tables. Despite this shortage there was always a determined effort to celebrate Christmas in a suitable manner and make it the outstanding festival of the year. Such a spirit was manifest by the first settlers in Rockport Ward in Summit Stake.

The few families who moved to that region had taken but few cattle with them that season. At Christmastime they prepared a cooperative or community dinner. In the Church record we read that "the men jointly purchased a piece of beef for which they agreed to pay in grain after the following harvest."

Thus was the spirit of Christmas kept alive by the pioneers, no matter how limited their resources were.

Improvement Era, December 1941, pp. 724f. E. Cecil McGavin, a native of Ashton, Idaho, received his B.A. and M.A. degrees from Brigham Young University and the University of Utah, respectively. An instructor in the LDS seminaries and institutes, he has written seventeen books on scriptures and Church history.

Jenny's Letter

BERNICE BROWN

Ovid, Idaho
Christmas Eve, 1943

Dear son:

It is so near Christmas here at the ranch that I can almost see the bells standing on tiptoe waiting to ring in the festive day. Evelyn has spent half the evening popping corn, and as fast as it grows into a curly white mound, Bobby sticks in his fist and neatly rations it. I don't know what she would do if you were here snitching too.

The tree looks like bargain day at the Five and Ten. Little Elna supervised the decoration as always, and the china angels we've had since your first Christmas are kept busy dodging the hodgepodge of candy canes and paper chains. Elna was delighted with the results and has just bounced up to bed. I expect to see her sliding down the banister at dawn and racing with flushed cheeks to the fireplace for the purely scientific purpose of determining the cause of her stocking's bulges. . . .

Dad's rubber boots are irrigating the rag rug by the stove. They have more patches on them than our tires. He's just come from the barn. Your heifer wisely chose this holy night to give birth to her first calf, a fine little bull. Dad says she seems quite pleased with herself, and she was smugly lapping the wobbly little fellow with her tongue.

The snow is quite deep this year. As I sit here writing, the wet white flakes are pressing damp faces against the window-pane. The window where your service star hangs is bright with holly. I wish I could send you a few sprigs for your submarine. . . .

Elna begged to play the piano while we sang the carols. Her Christmas spirit invaded the keys and camouflaged the technical errors. Silence filled the places where you used to come ringing in on the tenor. I filled these silences with the echoes of your voice from the first childish warblings to the time when we all smiled (secretly, of course) as your voice was trying to leap the hurdles from childhood to manhood, when it was a succession of squeaks and bass rumbles. . . .

I remembered the last Christmas you were here. That was when your best girl joined our family sing. Your newly given diamond made a brave sparkle on her finger; tiny snow diamonds still clung to her damp curls, but the bravest, sweetest sparkle of all was in the shining depths of her eyes. . . .

Last year you didn't receive our presents. You wrote saying you didn't mind that so much . . . just knowing we had sent them was enough.

Christmas will be as faded as the robes of our china angels when this letter reaches you. But tonight I feel that you will know that I'm writing it. You must know that, though we miss you, we are proud of what you have chosen to do.

So on this evening of our Savior's birth we are waiting at home for you to bring peace on earth.

All my love and a prayer,
Your mother

Improvement Era, December 1943, p. 243.

Uncle Kees' Christmas Rebellion

PIERRE VAN PAASSEN

During my boyhood in Holland, Christmas was by no means a joyous celebration. Our spiritual leaders clung to the interpretation handed down by that gloomiest of men, John Calvin. Even the singing of carols was considered tantamount to blasphemy, and festive candles and gaily decorated fir trees were deemed pagan abominations.

But one old-fashioned Calvinist Christmas lingers in my mind with delight. It was bitter cold in the great church that morning, for the vast nave and transept were unheated. Worshipers pulled the collars of their overcoats up around their chins and sat with their hands in their pockets. Women wrapped their shawls tightly around their shoulders. When the congregation sang, their breath steamed up on faint white clouds toward the golden chandeliers. The preacher that day was a certain Dr. van Hoorn, who was a representative of the ultra-orthodox faction.

The organist had sent word to my Uncle Kees that he was too ill to fulfill his duties. Kees, happy at the opportunity to play the great organ, now sat in the loft peering down through the curtains on the congregation of about 2,000 souls. He had taken me with him into the organ loft.

The organ, a towering structure, reached upward a full 125 feet. It was renowned throughout the land and indeed throughout all Europe. Its wind was provided by a man treading over a huge pedal consisting of twelve parallel beams.

In his sermon Dr. van Hoorn struck a pessimistic note. Christmas, he said, signified the descent of God into the tomb of human flesh, "that charnel house of corruption and dead bones." He dwelt sadistically on our human depravity, our utter worthlessness, tainted as we were from birth with original sin. The dominie groaned and members of the congregation bowed their heads in awful awareness of their guilt.

As the sermon progressed Kees grew more and more restless. He scratched his head and tugged at his mustache and goatee. He could scarcely sit still.

"Man, man," he muttered, shaking his head, "are these the good tidings, is that the glad message?" And turning to me he whispered fiercely, "That man smothers the hope of the world in the dustbin of theology!"

We sang a doleful psalm by way of interlude, and the sermon, which had already lasted an hour and forty minutes, moved toward its climax. It ended in so deep a note of despair that across the years I still feel a recurrence of the anguish I then experienced. It was more than likely, the minister threw out by way of a parting shot, that of his entire congregation not a single soul would enter the kingdom of heaven. Many were called, but few were chosen.

Kees shook with indignation as the minister concluded. For a moment I feared that he could walk off in a huff and not play the Bach postlude, or any postlude at all. Down below, Dr. van Hoorn could be seen lifting his hands for the benediction. Kees suddenly threw off his jacket, kicked off his shoes, and pulled out all the stops on the organ. When the minister had finished there followed a moment of intense silence.

Kees waited an instant longer while the air poured into the instrument. His face was set and grim and he looked extremely pale. Then throwing his head back and opening his mouth as if he were going to shout, he brought his fingers down on the keyboard. *Hallelujah! Hallelujah! Hallelujah!*

The organ roared the tremendous finale of Handel's chorus of *Messiah*. And again with an abrupt crashing effect, as if a million voices burst into song, *Hallelujah! Hallelujah! Hallelujah!* The music swelled and rolled with the boom of thunder against the vaulted dome, returning again and again with the blast of praise like breakers bursting on the seashore.

Kees beckoned to me. "More air!" he called out.

I ran into the bellows chamber, where Leendert Bols was stamping down the beams like a madman, transported by the music, waving his arms in the air.

"More air!" I shouted. "He wants more air!"

"Hallelujah!" Leendert shouted back. "Hallelujah!" He grabbed me by the arm and together we fairly broke into a trot on the pedal beams.

Then the anthem came to a close. But Kees was not finished yet. Now the organ sang out sweetly the Dutch people's most beloved evangelical song: "The Name above every Name, the Name of Jesus," sung to a tune very similar to "Home, Sweet Home."

We sang it with all our heart, Leendert and I, as did the congregation on its way out.

It was a tornado of melody that Kees had unleashed. Mountains leaped with joy. The hills and the seas clapped their hands in gladness. Heaven and earth, the voices of men and angels, seemed joined in a hymn of praise to a God who did not doom and damn, but who so loved, loved, loved the world.

Pierre Van Paassen, "Earth Could Be Fair," Dial Press (New York: Dell Publishing Company), as condensed in *Reader's Digest*, December 1946, pp. 57-58. Used by permission.

Peace on Earth

MARGUERITE JOHNSON GRIFFIN

It was the day before Christmas, and Jim Brock walked slowly with leaden feet out of the employees' entrance belonging to the large firm of Morton Furniture Manufacturers. His head was down. His worn and shapeless hat dropped over eyes which had lost all luster of happiness, over eyes in which lay the strain of despair. . . .

Christmas Eve! He must go home bearing a pay envelope which contained a paltry fifteen dollars, knowing that that must last until he could get another job. And how long would that be? How long must that money be made to buy food, warmth, and shelter for his little brood?

There was Sally who would graduate from high school in June, if only he could keep her going. Sally, gentle, loving, and talented, whose nimble fingers were those of the artist. If he could just provide for her the chance in life that she deserved and was soon to be ready for, art school. He sighed. No job. Where could he get another?

There was Bob, just starting high school. . . . Bob who rose early and studied late in order that he might deliver the morning paper as well as the evening news just so that he might have his books and a few clothes like the other fellows. And all because he, his father, could not make enough to provide everything for him. His shoulders sagged. . . .

Then there was little five-year-old Dan who would be wondering why Santa Claus would not bring him the electric train he wanted so much. Poor little Dan! . . . A tired, sad smile crossed his worried face as he recalled to his mind the picture of his wife sitting with little Dan upon her lap.

"You see, Danny," she had said gently. "Times have been very bad. And you know that Santa Claus spends all his days and most of his nights thinking of how he can make people happy, and because of that he has always neglected his business. Therefore, if men who spend all their time making money have felt the depression, don't you think Santa Claus who has spent more thought on little children than on making money—don't you think he, too, would have a hard time to provide everybody with as fine toys as he has before?"

"Yes, I guess so," little Danny had said wistfully, still unable to truly grasp what part money has to play in this big world of ours. "But Mummy," he went on earnestly, "I wouldn't mind if it wasn't a very big train. Just a little one would be all right. Or it really needn't be electric, either, if that's too much. One of those you wind up would be fun. Do you suppose he could manage that, Mummy? I wouldn't ask for nothin' else."

The man's expression of despair deepened into worn furrows upon his tired face. Until this very morning he, too, had been almost sure that Santa could manage the train, but now with heavy heart he plodded onward. . . .

To his discouraged ears came the tinkle of cheery Christmas bells. He stopped by a window full of toys. His eyes lighted. His pulses quickened. There it was! An electric train, with bright headlights, speeding rapidly around its winding course. It was not a big one, nor elaborate, but how it would gladden the heart of little Dan. He sighed and shrugged. It was impossible now. . . .

His feet were almost numb with the damp and cold. He would be glad to get home by his fire. It was only a block now, for he was passing the little church which was so near their small home. In its yard he noticed there had been erected since morning a big sign, decorated appropriately and effectively, with large letters proclaiming the age-old inscription: "Peace on earth, good will to men."

What a mockery for churches to flaunt such a thought before the eyes of men. There was no peace on earth. There was no good will among men. . . .

He was on his own porch now. He could hear the merry laughter of his children from within, while at intervals his wife's mellow voice mingled with theirs. She had been a sweet, brave woman, he thought, while his heart softened somewhat, then hardened bitterly again as he reminded himself of the news he had to tell her. That would put an end to their gay laughter, he thought as he vigorously stamped his feet upon the tiny porch.

In response Anna opened the door to him, surrounded by their merry bunch, Sally and Bob at right and left with little Dan peeking through first one opening and then another. They grabbed his arms, showered him with kisses, and ushered him into a room festively decorated with red and green streamers and Santa Claus cutouts. He sat down limply in the chair they offered him.

"Where in the world did you—" he started to say, but was interrupted by a chorus of voices.

"We didn't spend a single cent, Daddy," they exclaimed gleefully, while their well-meant words smote his heart because of his inability to provide them a better living.

"No," Sally went on. "My art teacher gave me a lot of this colored paper. Of course some of it is kind of old, but it doesn't look so bad, do you think?"

"It looks great," the man said. "You are all good children. But I've lost my job," he finished, each word brutally distinct.

For a moment there was silence.

"I've still got my paper routes. Two of them," interposed Bob, meaning to be encouraging.

"I want you to save your money for college, son," the man said tersely.

"I have been," the boy returned. "Practically every cent, so I guess I can give some to the best dad in the world if I want to."

"You are a good lad," said the father deeply moved, "but I don't think it will be that bad."

"I know it won't," said Anna in her calm, sure way. "It has been like this before, but something has always come along to keep us from ever being reduced to dire want. Don't worry, Jim."

"Things are getting better, too, Daddy," reassured Sally. "From what people are saying, I don't think it will be so hard this time." . . .

"See, Dad," said Sally, "I've made a Christmas card for Mother."

"It is beautiful," murmured the man, as he beheld there, drawn by the hand of his daughter and colored attractively, a picture of the Savior extending his arms to a weeping man and woman. What depths of understanding, meekness, comfort, and love she had portrayed on the face of Jesus, and what sorrow upon the countenances of the two who were seeking his blessing. It held the man almost spellbound. To think that his daughter's hand—

He read the inscription beneath it: "Blessed are they that mourn, for they shall be comforted."

"It is beautiful," he said. "But whom is it for?"

"Mama asked me to make it to send to Mr. and Mrs. Morton. They lost their little son two or three days ago."

"You shan't do it!" the man declared firmly and bitterly.

"Why, Daddy!" the girl breathed in dismay.

"What's all this?" asked the mother, coming in from the kitchen.

"She shan't send this card to those people," he explained harshly. "He fired me. They're rich, while we're in want. They—"

"Did he fire you personally?" asked the woman quietly.

"No, but he's at the head. He owns the concern."

"He probably doesn't even know who you are," his wife went on. "And anyway, during this Christmas season there is supposed to prevail good will in our hearts for all mankind and—"

"And on earth peace, I suppose," the man snapped ironically.

"Yes," she returned, puzzled at his outburst.

"Well, there is no peace anywhere. The injustice of our whole scheme of things drives out peace from even our very souls." His bitterness startled her.

"Never mind about that, then," his wife said softly. "Do you remember that day, only six years ago, when we—"

Her words summoned before his memory the face of their five-year-old Alice, stilled by the hand of death, and an expression of pain crossed his worn face.

"I remember," he said gently.

"And do you remember," she persisted, "how we learned that trust in the Savior and a knowledge of his plan of salvation was the only way to obtain a philosophy that was big enough to enable us to rise above our grief?"

"Yes, I remember," he repeated. "You are right as you always are. You must send the card. But you have no stamps. You told me to get some. I forgot."

"We won't spend money for stamps now. Sally and Bob and I will leave it in their mailbox. I've been in all day. I'll enjoy the walk."

That evening they trudged through the rapidly falling snow on past their own humble neighborhood into districts more prosperous and still more prosperous until they reached the Mortons' big home, big but empty because a little boy was no longer there to play within its walls. Anna wiped a tear from her eye. Well she knew and understood the aching hearts which were housed within. . . .

Until his wife and two other children came home, Jim walked his perturbed way, becoming worn out with exhaustion, so much so that it did not take long for his wife's gentle urgings and soothing words to entice him to bed and lull him off to sleep. One could not be too utterly discouraged around her. She had a way with you.

He was surprised that he had slept so soundly, but he was not disturbed until Dan's glee over a few ten-cent and home-made toys awakened the household. The man's mind once more bestirred itself to the realization that little Dan was doomed to disappointment. He threw his worn and faded bathrobe about his shoulders and rushed out to comfort the child.

But the little boy was looking between, in, and around everything stowed away beneath the tree which was decorated with tinsel and balls that sadly betrayed their age.

Then the child stood back and announced calmly: "My train has not come yet."

The mother and father exchanged bewildered looks. Then the man began to explain.

"Well, sonny, I'm afraid—"

"Oh, Daddy, you don't need to be. I know Santa is going to bring me one. I prayed about it last night you know, and—" He searched for words. "Well, you know how when you pray, sometimes you just get the feeling so strong that you know your prayer will be answered."

Tears were wet in the eyes of all, and for a long time no one spoke to break the magic of that moment. And so that Christmas Day was hallowed by the gift of the Divine Spirit which only the faith of a little child can impart. The simple homemade gifts which were exchanged were glorified by a greater family love and appreciation for each other, and perhaps the little sister who was missing from their presence enriched the morning with a tie that was spiritual.

It was a grateful and joyous family which unitedly partook of their simple Christmas dinner prepared by the capable hands of their mother, but late in the afternoon their gaiety was hushed by the ringing of the door bell.

The father said, "I'll go," and they were all surprised to hear him say, "Why, come in, Mr. and Mrs. Morton."

The children clustered wide-eyed in the background while their mother with gentle courtesy and simple hospitality offered them chairs and took their wraps.

"We just wanted to drop in, Mr. and Mrs. Brock," said Mr. Morton, "to thank you for the lovely card we received from you this morning."

"You don't know what it has meant to me," Mrs. Morton said gently, while tears threatened to fill her eyes. "I can't say more."

"You don't need to," answered the mother. "I know exactly how you feel. I've been through it, too."

Mr. Morton went on. "You don't know what it has done to our very house, that exquisite little painting and those holy words. It has brought a warmth that we haven't known since— since—" Words failed him. Then he gained control of himself and said, "Who painted it?"

"Our daughter here," the father answered proudly, bringing forward the girl who blushed timidly.

"She has talent. I would like to do something for her. Have you ever thought of going to art school?"

"Oh, yes," she spoke up eagerly. "But I doubt if I will be able to. Times have been so poor for us and Daddy has lost his job."

"Yes, yes. I know about that, too. When your card came I couldn't place you, so I had my secretary look you up. You will come to work in the morning. I need a man like you, for a man with such children as these, with such happiness in their faces when you have so little, is the man I want for a special job I have in mind, which will give more pay and a chance for advancement." He went on hurriedly, ignoring the man's attempted thanks. "And, young lady, I am going to send you to art school. Oh, your father will soon be making enough to do that for you himself, but I want the honor."

The girl was speechless with joy. "I can't thank you enough."

"Don't try, for we can't thank you either," he said and abruptly turned to Bob. "Young man, I need an energetic boy like you in my office afternoons after school. It will pay more than even two paper routes and you won't have to get up so early in the morning." He finished with an understanding twinkle in his eye.

"Gee, that's swell," Bob breathed.

"And you, my son," he said, turning to Dan. "For you there is an electric train. We have no little boy to play with it now, and we thought you might like it."

"Would I? Didn't I tell you? Didn't I tell you?" cried the child, running in excited circles while Mr. Morton went out to his car and brought in and set up the most elaborate train outfit that the boy had ever seen. And the bereft rich man and woman stayed for several hours, enjoying the excitement and pleasure of the little boy who had known his train would come.

Finally they arose to go. . . . After hearty good-byes had been said, Anna and Jim stood in the doorway watching their kind new friends get into the luxurious car which stood waiting at the curb. Jim placed his arm around Anna's waist affectionately, and she smiled up at him.

"You see, dear," she said, "God is ever mindful of us as he is of all his children. All he asks of us is courage to face life and its problems the best we can, and faith in his wisdom and justice."

"Yes," responded the man. "We must have faith as strong and implicit as that of our little Dan and courage like his which remained undaunted even though his train was not in the expected place at the expected time, for his faith gave him the assurance that his reward would come, and he was patient. Bless our children," he finished almost under his breath.

Relief Society Magazine, December 1934, pp. 733-39. Note: This story is fiction.

This Blessed Christmas Day

DRUCILLA H. McFARLAND

t must have been a long time that we had been ill.

My sister Eleanor and I were in the same bed. Across the room were Estella and Beatrice. Out in the large living room I could see Joseph and William in a bed on the floor. They were only staying in it occasionally, meantime slipping around to tease us girls.

Sadie, the eldest, was up and about now and helping our mother.

"It's just like you children to all come down at once with measles. Then Joe gets out for one day and comes back with chicken pox to start all around the circle again," Ma complained good-naturedly. She took the tin washbasin from Bea and handed her a towel and comb and then stopped before Stella. Joe slipped behind her and put one of Pinkie's new kittens on top of her head, nearly causing the upset of the water.

"Young man," Ma scolded, "would you like a taste of thimble pie for your breakfast this morning?" (A rap with a thimbled finger.)

"I'd like anything, Ma, that's different from flummity."

Bea wailed, "Are we going to have that brown flour mush again?"

Ma's eyes filled with tears and she turned quickly to put another stick into the round pot-bellied iron stove.

"Tomorrow is Christmas," Joe said. "I'll bet if Pa was here—"

"Where is Pa?" little Eleanor queried. Sadie put her arms around Eleanor, looking very sad too, since Ma had gone outside and closed the door softly to cry all by herself.

"Ellie," Sadie said to this little sister, "Pa has just gone on another mission."

"That's what Ma says, but it has been so long."

"Longer even than last time," Bea said. She was hardly old enough to realize that this mission would be endless. She remembered and wanted the joyousness of his last return from the Church mission in Tennessee. She wanted to forget how the neighbor children hurt her by telling her, "Forget the mission story. Your father got killed building the Weber bridge."

Mother, coming back in, asked Will if he thought he could walk to the big hill and cut a tall cedar for our Christmas tree. Of course he could.

She brought popcorn she had raised and set Gideon Junior and me to preparing it for the girls to make strands of decorations, with the understanding that we were not to eat too much of it.

Our meal of flummity and milk was just finished the next morning when we heard sleigh bells. Joe pulled back the curtain that mother kept over the window to protect our measle-sore eyes from the light. "Ma, it's a man with a sleighload of . . ."

Mother answered the knock at our door and the man walked in carrying a shank of beef.

Before she could frame her speech of rejection he said, "No use to say 'no,' Sister Holmes. This is my privilege of having a happy Christmas by giving one."

Our mother knew that this good man believed every word he spoke. He was William McFarland. His Scottish father's family and her Scottish father John Martin were close neighbors in pioneering the new town of West Weber.

"But I have no money to pay," Mother said.

"Sister Holmes, that's the reason I am here. Just enjoying my privilege of helping the widows and the fatherless."

"But I have never accepted charity from anyone before."

"That I know, too, and my wish is that you need not again. But now, Merry Christmas and may God bless you all! Good day."

We could think of roast, gravy, suet pudding!

Ma got out the skillet while Joe whittled thin chips from the frozen round of beef, and we sat down to our second breakfast that morning. Mother said, "William, you ask the blessing."

Will, just coming sixteen, was the man of the house now, and he could offer a proper prayer of thanks. He said the words aloud, and everyone of us repeated them in our hearts, saying aloud: "We thank Thee, Heavenly Father, for this blessed Christmas Day. Amen."

Deseret News, December 19, 1972, p. 1. Reprinted by permission. Drucilla Holmes McFarland was born in Wilson, Weber County, Utah, in 1891, and attended the Weber Academy in Ogden, Utah. In 1914 she married Archibald J. McFarland, and they became the parents of six children. He died in 1967. Sister McFarland was Weber County Mother of the Year in 1959. The event she described in this story took place in 1896.

On Christmas Morning

SYLVIA YOUNG

When I awoke, sunlight was filtering through the venetian blinds of the window next to my bed. Still half asleep and startled by the unfamiliarity of the room, I couldn't remember just where I was for the moment, but the pungent smell of anesthetics and a nurse in a crisp, white uniform, walking across the corridor, brought me back to reality. From somewhere down the hall came the soft strains of "Hark! the Herald Angels Sing." I was in a hospital bed, and it was Christmas morning.

I hadn't wanted to be hospitalized for Christmas. There was so much I had planned for the day with our two small boys —so much I would have to miss.

The nurse looked in from the doorway. "Merry Christmas," she said. "You're looking good. Everything okay?"

I nodded. "I'm fine, but I surely hadn't planned being here today."

She laughed. "Nobody wants to be in the hospital on Christmas, but it isn't so bad. We're really festive. Wait until you see our trees, and the cute favors for your breakfast trays."

Right then I wasn't thinking of Christmas trees or favors. "When will they bring the babies?" I asked.

"Oh, you mothers," she exclaimed. "How about right after breakfast?"

Warm, and sweet smelling, with soft, black hair crowning his wee head, I thought he looked something like an angel when the nurse brought him in to me. A boy—a third little boy, born on Christmas morning. So much I had wanted a daughter, but now it didn't matter at all. Carefully, I opened the tight closed small fist and looked at the perfectly formed, tiny hand. Birth. What a great miracle, work of a master creator, and I had been privileged to play a part in it!

The sweet music of "Silent Night" came from the room next door, and as I listened to the song my thoughts went back across the wide centuries to a lowly stable in Bethlehem where a young Jewish maiden, chosen of God, birthed the little Christ Child on the hay.

I looked around the warm, modern hospital room—what a contrast to the crude, cold abode that Mary had known. How different my baby's sleeping place than the Holy Child's manger bed! And yet, on that beautiful Christmas morning, when a great spiritual peace filled my whole being, and I felt especially close to the Lord, I knew that my feelings of humility and gratitude were much the same as hers must have been. Although she was the mother of the Lord Jesus, I had been blessed to bear other children of God—two little boys at home, and now their baby brother—a special Christmas gift.

In that quiet hour, in the presence of a little child who had so recently come from the home of the Creator, I meditated on the meaning of Christmas and the miracle of life. This was a hospital, and every day there was birth and death here, but death was not the end. Life was everlasting. He, the Savior of the world, with his atoning sacrifice, had bought this gift for us, the greatest of all gifts—the gift of life eternal.

This was Christmas, a time to give thanks, to remember. And there in the morning stillness my spirit was in tune with the Infinite.

Since then many Christmases have come and gone, and the boy born that morning is a man now. But whenever I bring out the Christmas decorations, I spend a quiet moment of reflection

as I unwrap a small ornament—three tiny wax Christmas carolers, the favor on my breakfast tray that Christmas morning
in the hospital twenty-seven years ago. And I think that Christmas will always be the one I remember best, not only because
it is the birthday of a son, but because, away from the hurry and
worry of getting and giving, I had time for spiritual rejuvenation
in the beautiful remembering of our Lord's nativity and its great
promise for us all—the true meaning of Christmas, which is so
often forgotten in our materialistic world.

Deseret News, December 21, 1971, p. 1. Reprinted by permission. Sylvia Young
and her husband, Reid W. Young, reside in Midvale, Utah. A writer of poetry and
short stories, she has had many of her writings published in Church publications,
and has won awards in the Relief Society Magazine's Eliza R. Snow writing contests.

Katie's Prayer

GRANT ALLYN CAPRONI

It was nearly dark when Loring MacBride stopped in front of his house. A heavy fog filled the cold wet air, adding gloom to his depressed spirits. In and out of office buildings in the congested business district and through sparsely settled sections to various industrial plants he had tramped through slush and snow all the day, seeking work, with always the same response. "We're laying men off instead of taking them on." And, "Sorry, but we have nothing to offer." . . .

And Christmas only three weeks away! What would he say to . . . Katie who lived the whole year waiting for Christmas? . . .

Stoically he strode into the house, his senses benumbed from unending thinking, anxiety, and misery, and with no word of greeting, his face expressionless. . . . Mrs. MacBride and the two little daughters were huddled about the kitchen stove, the family rendezvous since they left off using the furnace.

"Here's Dad," greeted Mrs. MacBride, smiling up into his face. Katie clung to him, and little Martha's first words were to inquire if he had seen Santa Claus. . . .

MacBride removed his overcoat and sank heavily into a chair by the stove. His elbows went to his knees and his chin to his palms. No one talked as the children helped their mother

set the table. What a different home from this time last year!
The shouts of joy which had gone up when he entered the house
after work, and the deluge of Christmas prattle. Now the parlor
was dark and cold. The fireplace had not been lighted this winter. Where were the childish decorations and laughter and letters to Santa Claus? . . . Mrs. MacBride kissed away a lone
forbidden tear and whispered something to him.

"Dad, do you remember," asked Katie suddenly, "the time
I prayed that the lights would come on again in that awful
storm, and sure enough they did?"

"And we're going to have a Christmas and Santa will surely
come," interposed little Martha.

"Dad," Katie went on, "do you remember the time they
made you talk in church and you said you knew God answered
prayers? You still believe it, don't you?"

"Yes, darling, when it's for the best. Of course, sometimes
we are carried away by our impulses and ask for things we
later see would not have been right, and then God has to get us
straightened out again."

"Is it right to ask for Santa to come?"

"Yes, darling. Yes, Katie."

. . . Each morning Mr. MacBride would go forth searching
for work. He no longer confined himself to his own profession
as he sought work, but would inquire wherever likelihood of
employment was possible. . . .

He had not gone far from the warehouse when he was
hailed by a hearty young voice. Harry Holler drove up to the
curb, stopped short, and threw a leg over the Ford door. He once
took mechanical drawing in MacBride's class in one of the local
high schools.

"Say, Mac, I was coming over to see you tonight. I want to
get your advice on something. I have a couple of offers and I'm
stuck which to take."

A shadow crossed Mac's face. . . . The lad rattled on while
Mac meditated. After he had finished and MacBride had duly
weighed the facts as presented, he advised him the position to
accept. "If I remember correctly, you took less than a half a year
in the three-year drafting course, or was it in the four-year one?"

"The four-year course."

"And have you had any further training or experience since?"

"No, Mac, I haven't."

"Well, Harry, how do you get these jobs? I have been to both of those firms and they told me they had nothing in sight."

"I'll tell you how it is, Mac. Both of the men who are offering me these jobs owe my dad political debts, and that is the way they want to pay them off."

MacBride walked dejectedly down the street. . . .

Returning home early that afternoon, he entered the basement. . . . He went into the provision room. There were a scant few bottles of fruit left over from the year before last. He turned to the coal bin. Would the coal hold out till after Christmas?

That night MacBride went into the children's bedroom to hear their bedtime prayers. Little Martha's first utterance was to ask God to send Santa Claus, and Katie prayed too for Santa to come, laying before the Lord her reasons why he should be sent, what he should bring, and that he must not forget Mrs. Cox, who was always doing a kind deed for others. "And Father," concluded little Katie, "will leave the front door unlocked so Santa can get in with a big pack, and don't forget the poor blind lady on Seventh street."

Early in the morning of the day before Christmas it began to snow, and by noon the landscape lay under a heavy blanket of white. There were muffled sounds of voices passing in the street. Once a horse went trotting by with two sleds hitched behind. Mrs. MacBride could make out two figures on the sled, and the horse's sleighbells made a soft faraway sound. She made molasses candy and baked some cakes and cookies, after which she gave a few final touches to two small dresses she had made out of her wedding dress. . . . Tonight would be Christmas. . . . What would she do Christmas morning when the children ran into the parlor? Would they stop short at the door, unable to believe their eyes? No tree! Empty stockings! There would be two little parcels done up in newspaper and a dish of miserable molasses candy on the mantel! . . .

"What does all this mean?" It was Mrs. Ash, who had

walked quietly in. Mr. MacBride had often declared that Mrs. Ash was a good luck sign, and Mrs. MacBride inwardly rejoiced at the sight of her good neighbor.

Mrs. MacBride said little, but the discerning eye of Mrs. Ash saw much.

"Well," said the good neighbor, "I don't know how it will happen, but I feel that it will all come out all right, somehow."

It was with renewed hope that Mrs. MacBride got to her feet after Mrs. Ash had gone. . . . At the supper table Katie gradually sensed the situation. Both parents were looking down at their plates when Katie spoke.

"Don't feel bad, Mother. . . . We've said our prayers, you know." . . .

It is almost morning. . . . Mrs. MacBride has not so much as dozed for an instant. . . . She listens to the heavy troubled breathing of her husband. . . .

Listen! What was that? Has the time come? Are the children slipping into the parlor? She raises on an elbow. The children's room is dark and still. Gratefully she drops back on her comfortless pillow. Listen! Surely that is a noise. She raises her head slightly. Involuntarily her breathing stops. Someone is walking in stocking feet. . . . She sits upright. . . . The crevice between the parlor door and its jamb discloses a light. . . . Panic-stricken, she is about to rouse her husband, but another sound arrests her attention—the unmistakable whine of a mama-doll. She struggles to throw the thought out of her mind. How foolish to believe! The inevitable disappointment to follow will be more than she can stand. . . .

A switch snaps. The light in the crevice is brighter. Cautiously Mrs. MacBride slips over the foot of the bed and peers through the keyhole. Sure enough, someone is filling the stockings. Now he has turned partly her way. He is smiling and chuckling as he surveys his work. The switch snaps again, leaving the room utterly dark. Then a great hoarse shout rends the night air: "Merry Christmas! Merry Christmas!" The front door slams. Loring MacBride springs to his feet. Mrs. MacBride throws her arms about him and . . . sobbing tells him Santa has come and Katie's prayers are answered. Together they steal into the room, switching on the light and looking back to make sure the children are not awake. Speechless, they look upon a beautiful tree with mounds of parcels, packages, bundles and toys heaped about it. MacBride is first to recover. He steps up to the tree and takes hold of an envelope. There is writing on both sides of it. "Do not open until after breakfast." Mrs. MacBride moves toward one corner of the room. There, in a heap, are groceries, a dressed turkey, and everything to go into a Christmas dinner.

At breakfast they open and read the letter:

Dear Sir:

On my way down from the North Pole I ran into an old pal of yours. He told me all about you—how he strolled into your office years ago when you were a young engineer just starting out for yourself and he laid before you his idea of a new pumping engine he had invented. He asked you if it would work. You said "Yes." "Then," said he, "would you be willing to go ahead and design such an engine, involving this principle of hydraulics, and take your chances of pay on my sometime getting it patented and on the market?" You said "Yes." And he told me how you struggled day after day and night after night with plans and little hope of pay—and for a man you had never seen before. Night before last when you went in to hear Katie's prayer I happened by. Wasn't that providential? Now, sir, there is a position open for an engineer with half interest in the company that will market that engine. That's all I'm authorized to say except that your pal said to tell you he would eat Christmas dinner with you and then he would tell you all about it.

Merry Christmas and Happy New Year,
Santa Claus

Improvement Era, December 1930, pp. 83-85 ff. Note: This story is fiction.

A Christmas Gift for the Doctor

JOHN COLLINS HARVEY

It is in his first year of actually practicing medicine that full realization dawns on the young doctor of the tremendous responsibility for human life placed in his hands. Believe me, this can be quite frightening. Grave doubts arise in the young intern's mind about his knowledge, ability, and worthiness. Wise guidance from more experienced physicians, coupled with the appreciation and affection shown him by patients he has helped, builds self-confidence. But the process is a slow one.

My own doubts were so great in the fall of my internship year at Johns Hopkins Hospital that I had about decided to leave medicine for another field. But fate intervened.

One Saturday morning in September a thirty-nine-year-old woman, Irene by name, was brought to the hospital. She was a pitiful creature, emaciated, woebegone, looking twice her age. Her family, who had driven her to Baltimore from their small farm on the Eastern Shore of Maryland in their twenty-year-old truck, were obviously very poor.

Irene talked irrationally at times, fidgeting with the bedclothes, pulling at her hair. Her family reported that she had been getting "peculiar" for some time. She didn't eat and had become so weak that she had taken to her bed and showed no interest in her surroundings. A doctor had told them she was mentally ill and should be committed to the state hospital, but they decided to bring her to Baltimore to see if she couldn't be helped.

That afternoon the resident physician and I examined her. We found that she was suffering from a profound anemia, a heart condition, and severe overactivity of the thyroid gland. She was started on iodine drops for hyperthyroidism. Digitalis was given for her heart. An X-ray of her stomach, taken the next day, showed a large ulcer, and treatment was instituted. She was given blood transfusions and fed intravenously for a few days.

Gradually Irene became quiet. She began to eat. Her heart began to function more efficiently. Her anemia disappeared, and she became quite a different person.

I got to know her well during this time. She had little formal schooling and knew virtually nothing about the world beyond the Eastern Shore. But she was endowed with a great deal of common sense and was rich in her love for people. I spent many spare moments at her bedside, listening to her talk about life on the farm, crops, cooking, or her family. She loved flowers, but since the family had no land to spare for growing anything but food, she would pick wild flowers in the fields, and tree blossoms. One of her favorites was holly, which grew around her home.

Finally the day came for Irene's discharge. She shook hands with me and said simply, "Thank you, Doc."

We arranged for her to be cared for by a physician on the Eastern Shore, since she had no money to come back for periodic checkups. Anyway, traveling from her home and getting about in Baltimore would be too confusing for her, she thought. The physician sent word on several occasions that she was doing well, and in the press of work I did not think much more about Irene.

Then Christmas approached. The wards were decorated; the quiet of Christmas Eve descended. After dinner that evening I went over to the administration building where, each Christmas Eve for nearly half a century, the choir of the Memorial Baptist Church has sung carols for the staff. There was the sparkle of anticipation in the air. People away from home and loved ones, each alone with his own problems, yet all bound together in the common work of caring for the sick, stood or sat on the balconies of the four-story central rotunda, waiting. On the main floor below, the choir, gowned in cassocks, prayed softly around the large marble statue of Christ, then burst into song.

The singing was magnificent, the scene was beautiful; yet I was terribly sad. This was my first Christmas away from home. I tried to concentrate on the singing, but doubts of my ability as a doctor, dissatisfaction with my own efforts, a feeling of unworthiness overcame me. Finally the choir was singing the "Hallelujah Chorus" from the *Messiah,* and it was over. The choir moved on to the wards to sing for the patients.

As I turned to go back to my ward, the porter at the front door beckoned to me. He handed me a box wrapped in brown paper, tied with a piece of red string. During the caroling, he said, a woman had slipped in and asked for me. He told her I was probably up on one of the balconies and he couldn't call me until the caroling was finished. She said she couldn't wait; she had only twenty minutes before the last bus left for home.

I took the package up to my room and opened it. Over the old brown paper were pasted Christmas decorations cut from newspapers. On one flap of the box was pasted half of an old Christmas card; it had a printed name, lined through with red crayon, and my name printed crudely on it instead. Inside the box were pieces of holly branches, obviously freshly picked.

I knew immediately who the donor was and why she couldn't wait. She had made the long, unaccustomed trip to Baltimore, and now had a four-hour bus ride back to the Eastern Shore to get home for Christmas!

Freshly picked holly in a crudely decorated carton tied with a knotted piece of red string. A simple present from a poor, uneducated woman—it was the greatest gift I have ever received. I looked out the window into the dark sky with its brightly shining stars. And I thought of that night some 1900 years ago. From a distance I heard the choir singing, "Bearing gifts, we traverse afar. . . ."

I knew then what I had wanted to know for some time.

Reprinted with permission from the *Saturday Evening Post,* copyright 1958, The Curtis Publishing Company; condensed from the *Reader's Digest,* December 1959, pp. 25-27.

The Perfect Christmas

BETTY LOU MARTIN SMITH

A blanket of fresh snow covered the ground, making the colonial-style home with the typical green shutters a picture for a Christmas card. Inside the cozy home, Judith Blair busied herself making cookies for the fast-approaching holiday season. Excitement filled the atmosphere in anticipation of the days to come.

My family will soon be home, Judith thought, as she worked, a glowing look of happiness upon her delicate face. She and her husband Henry had looked forward to the holiday season for so long. It would be the first time that the family had been together in three years. Steven, their son, had been stationed overseas with the Air Force, and Kathy, their daughter, was away at college in her sophomore year.

Judith remembered pleasantly the times that she and Kathy had spent together shopping for the holidays, and she could hardly wait until they could have that time together again. We've always been such a close family, she thought, and now there'll be just the four of us as it was before Steven went overseas.

Putting the cookies in the oven to bake, Judith walked over to the window. Outside, the shadows cast a strange, mystic light as the twilight came. The view was indeed breathtaking, and she breathed a sigh at its loveliness. It will be a perfect Christmas this year, she smiled contentedly to herself.

The ringing of the telephone brought Judith back to reality as she hurried to its beckoning.

"Hello, Mom, this is Kathy."

"Kathy!" Judith was surprised. "Is everything all right? I didn't expect to hear from you again before we met the train."

"Everything is just fine, Mom," Kathy explained. "I just wondered how you would like to have guests over the holidays. My two roommates, Sue and Angela, are going to be left here alone for the holidays. It is too far for them to go home; and I thought maybe it would seem more like Christmas to them if they spent it with us."

Judith was glad that Kathy couldn't see the disappointment on her face. "Kathy, I was planning on just the four of us spending the holidays together," she managed.

Kathy was silent for a moment. "Everyone needs a family at Christmas, Mom. I've already sort of asked them. I know that I should have called you and Daddy first."

Her composure regained, Judith added quickly, "Of course, dear, if that is what you want, then we will make the best of it."

"I know that you won't be sorry, Mother. You'll like the girls every bit as well as I do. I just know it." Kathy's voice was excited. "We'll see you in a couple of days."

"It sounds great to me," Henry Blair, a distinguished man with graying hair, said, as he hung his overcoat in the hall closet. "I like young people around, especially at Christmastime."

"I know where Kathy got her impulsiveness from, Henry." Judith was annoyed. "She never could turn away a stray cat or dog, and neither could you. She should think of her family before she acts."

For the first time Henry noticed the crushed look on his wife's face. Over the years he had come to know her every mood so well.

"You're disappointed that we are not going to be just the four of us this year, aren't you, dear?" Gently Henry put his arms around Judith.

The tears of disapproval finally gave way in Judith. "I thought this was going to be the best Christmas ever, and now Kathy's bringing the girls with her. I know that I sound selfish, Henry, but I did so want us to enjoy this Christmas."

"There's certainly no reason in the world why we can't enjoy Christmas as much this year as we ever have," Henry comforted his wife.

"I wish I had your compassion, Henry." Judith dried her eyes. "I'll do my best to make them feel welcome. I won't let Kathy down."

"That's my girl." Henry smiled. "I think that we should get them a present so they won't be left out on Christmas morning."

"Trust you to think of everything. Of course, we wouldn't want the girls to feel left out of things."

As Kathy had promised, the girls were very sweet and seemed to fit into the home exceptionally well. Even quiet, good-looking Steven was more jovial and talkative than usual.

Kathy's roommate, Sue, was small and brown-haired with an air of mischievousness about her, and the sprinkling of freckles across her upturned nose added to her charm. Angela, a lovely, dark-haired girl, was less talkative than Sue, but every bit as charming in her quiet way.

"Aren't they simply terrific, Mom?" Blue-eyed Kathy bubbled as she helped her mother in the kitchen. "And they think that the family is simply terrific, too."

"Yes, they are very nice, Kathy." Judith tried to sound convincing.

The day before Christmas dawned bright and crisp. The earth appeared as an enchanted fairyland with its sparkling white snow.

"What a simply glorious day to go shopping." Kathy went into Judith's room and found her seated in front of the window. "Aren't you ready, Mom? We're going in a few minutes."

"I didn't plan on going with you, Kathy." Judith turned her face away from her daughter. "You young people don't want me tagging along with you."

"Oh, but we do, Mrs. Blair." Angela stood in the doorway.

"It will be more like being at home having you with us. Please come."

"Please do, Mrs. Blair," Sue added as she walked up to the side of Angela. "It will be such fun."

A pleasant feeling came over Judith, and her face flushed becomingly. "Well, I guess that I might as well. It will only take me a few minutes to get ready." She was flattered that the girls would want her with them.

Judith couldn't remember having spent a happier day in her entire life. The girls were so congenial and such fun to be with. The Christmas carols sounded out joyously as they walked from store to store, and the sidewalk Santas added their warmth to the day.

"I can't ever remember having walked so far on campus," Sue commented, as she removed her shoes and flopped into an easy chair. "Mrs. Blair is the only one who doesn't seem tired at all. I honestly don't know how parents do it."

Angela and Kathy laughed. "I know that I can't keep up with them," Angela chided.

"I don't know whether I am going to be able to dance tonight or not," Kathy said weakly, "although it is very thoughtful of Steve to get us dates."

"Oh, come on now, Kathy. He just arranged it so that he could go with Angela," Sue teased.

"Honestly, Sue, I don't know where you get your ideas from." Angela blushed as she tried to match Sue's wit.

It was evident that Steven was quite taken by Angela. He had never been so attentive to a girl before. "I must say that Steven has good taste," Judith said approvingly.

Christmas Eve the girls took over little chores that had always tired Judith before, and she could not remember having felt so rested the day before Christmas. She went about her remaining tasks leisurely, enjoying every moment of her family's and guests' happy chatter. The very air had a mystery about it, as if it were truly about to proclaim the anniversary of the Savior's birth. How beautiful and tranquil the world seemed, and how beautiful and tranquil Judith felt in her heart.

That evening after supper, everyone gathered in the living

room to hear Henry's traditional reading from the Bible the story of the Savior's birth.

Kathy turned the Christmas tree lights on, and they flickered merrily in the warm light of the fireplace.

Judith let her gaze rest upon each of the faces before her, and she thought that she had never seen a more lovely sight. Each face had a glow about it that could only mean the love and peace that the spirit of Christmas brings to the very heart and soul. As Henry read from the Bible, there were tears in the eyes of each listener, and Judith turned away, her eyes also filled with tears. She knew that she could never again have a more beautiful experience or feel as she did at that moment.

After Henry had finished reading, there was a hushed silence about the room. It was Sue who broke the silence. "I guess you folks can't begin to realize what this means to Angela and me, being here with you. I feel just as though I were home. Thank you both so very much."

"That goes for me, too." Angela put her arms about Judith. "I do feel as though I were home."

"You are home, my dear." Judith really meant it. "And I want you to know that I can't remember a more perfect Christmas."

Relief Society Magazine, December 1965, pp. 896-99. Note: This story is fiction.

I Was Grateful Just to Be Alive

ROYAL R. MESERVY

It was the Sunday before Christmas, and our family was discussing memorable Christmases. After some discussions among the children, my eleven-year-old son Greg asked, "Dad, which Christmas do you remember best? Will you tell us about it?"

That was a big order, but after a few minutes' hesitation, I proceeded to tell them this experience:

The Christmas that stands out most in my mind was that of 1944, during World War II. We had fought through the Battle of the Ardennes and were then sent to the Siegfried Line to replace the Second Division. We had been there a week when the German offensive known as the Belgian Bulge began. We were right on the nose of that thrust and were commanded to hold at all costs. For two and a half days we fought and held. But finally, on December 19, 1944, we were forced to surrender.

After we were searched, we stood out in a barnyard all night. The next morning we began a march of thirty-eight miles. There was no food, except part of a raw sugar beet that I dashed into a field to get as we marched along.

The following morning, after sleeping on the cold, damp

ground, we moved slowly forward. We arrived at a big building about noon and were given two packages of German emergency ration crackers and a ride to the Geroldstein, Germany, railway station, where we slept on the hard cement. On December 21, we were loaded aboard a train of boxcars, with sixty-five men to each car. The sliding doors on either side of the car were wired shut from the outside. There was no food or water.

December 23, 1944, found us outside of Diez, still cramped up in the boxcar, hungry and thirsty. It was on this memorable afternoon that I learned the true meaning of Christmas.

Just before dark American bombers flew overhead, and bombs fell so close that one boxcar door was ripped entirely off. As the bombing continued, someone asked, "Has anybody got a Bible?" I reached into my pocket and handed him my pocket edition of the New Testament. He turned to the second chapter of Saint Luke and read:

"And there were in the same country shepherds abiding in the field, keeping watch over their flock by night.

"And, lo, the angel of the Lord came upon them, and the glory of the Lord shone round about them: and they were sore afraid.

"And the angel said unto them, Fear not: for, behold, I bring you good tidings of great joy, which shall be to all people.

"For unto you is born this day in the city of David a Saviour, which is Christ the Lord.

"And this shall be a sign unto you; Ye shall find the babe wrapped in swaddling clothes lying in a manger.

"And suddenly there was with the angel a multitude of the heavenly host praising God, and saying,

"Glory to God in the highest, and on earth peace, good will toward men." (Luke 2:8-14.)

I had heard that scripture read year after year, but never before or since with the emotion and feeling with which it was read in that boxcar.

Peace came over us. He handed the Bible back to me, and we all sat quietly, each deep in his own thoughts.

The next day, after eighty-eight hours without water, we

were given water and later some food. Christmas of 1944 is the one I remember best because I was grateful just to be alive.

Improvement Era, December 1970, p. 6. Dr. Royal R. Meservy, a native of Wilford Fremont County, Idaho, has served two full-time missions for the Church. He and his wife have seven children; the family resides in Fullerton, California, where he is a counselor at Fullerton College.

No Gifts?

MILTON L. WEILENMANN

From the vantage point of one's middle years it is exciting and stimulating to look back at the Mount Everests in our life—the high points of our existence—the lesson-makers of our mortality.

In 1960 our family experienced one of these high points. During the month of October I was called by President David O. McKay to preside over the Alaskan-Canadian Mission. It was newly organized, and no mission home existed. I was asked to find a suitable home, and a prayerful search of the great city of Vancouver, British Columbia, led me to a stately mansion on Connaught Drive. Built by a family prominent in the lumber and fishing industries in Canada, it was now unoccupied and darkened. Constructed along the lines of a great English manor house, the home had a ballroom that had witnessed receptions for two presidents of the United States and many prime ministers of Canada. Royalty had entered through its massive oak front door.

Yes, the family who owned it would sell it to the Church, but with one stipulation—it could not be occupied by its new owners until Christmas Eve, because on the 23rd of December, 1960, the family who had built the home and loved it wanted to come back to hold one final great dance in its ballroom. It would glitter once more for its original owners. We could have it on Christmas Eve, after the great men of Vancouver and their ladies had bade the home farewell.

Such a plan for purchase was agreeable to the Church, and on the night of the day before Christmas Eve the great ball was held. Five massive Christmas trees were placed in the home.

On the day before Christmas we moved in—my wife, six children, and I. Save for those five trees, a great dining table with eighteen chairs in the dining room, and four beds in the bedrooms, the house was vacant. Our furniture together with the gifts we had purchased for each other—all the usual things one has for the celebration of Christmas—were on a moving van somewhere between Salt Lake City and Vancouver. Suddenly we realized that even though the trees filled the house with the smell of pine, and holly red with berries grew profusely outside the front door, on the morrow no presents would be found under any of the resplendent Christmas trees. Were we to be forgotten on that Christmas Day?

When we awoke Christmas morning there really were no presents under the trees. We looked around and there were indeed no gifts. But that day we learned a lesson—and a great truth dawned. We conquered another Mount Everest and witnessed another high point in our lives. No gifts—yet we shared the greatest gift of all, and more than any one of us could open, hold, have, or enjoy in a single day. And what was it? It was ourselves, and the joy of being together, and sharing the wondrous story of Jesus together. We left the house and skipped together in a beautiful park, and looked up to a lazy sun that filtered through majestic pines. We even took our shoes off and dipped our feet in the Straits of Georgia, whose chill had been tempered by the warming Japanese current.

In the afternoon when the missionaries and Saints came, we sliced a big ham and enjoyed good food with our new friends. Afterwards, we sang again, and talked again, and prayed again!

Never in its most glittering days, never even in the presence of a prime minister, had that great old home known such joy or happiness. Never in its fifty or more years had the house seen such a marvelous Christmas . . . nor had we! And it was done without gifts, with nothing but each other, our friends, and the missionaries—and Jesus himself. For his spirit truly filled that house on that Christmas Day . . . which now seems so long ago!

Instructor, November 1970, p. 389. Milton L. Weilenmann is executive director of the Utah Department of Development Services. The father of seven children, he served as president of the Alaskan-Canadian Mission, 1960-63.

Home for Christmas

MYRTLE M. DEAN

Anne placed the two letters side by side on the desk. One letter was from her mother. The envelope was addressed in a hurried, sweeping hand. The letter inside was full of loving, newsy words. . . . "How glad we will be to have you home again. We can hardly wait to see the baby. It is wonderful that you will be back in America for Christmas," Anne's mother wrote. The second letter was from Bob's mother. It lay unopened, for Anne always left Bob's mail for him to read first, even though it was addressed to Mr. and Mrs. Robert Andrews. Anne knew that this letter would be as methodical and prim as the woman who wrote it. Bob's mother wrote with a meticulously neat and even hand. Anne smiled as she compared the two envelopes and looked over at her little son.

"Only ten more days and we will be back home in America, Jamie darling. Home for Christmas with Grandpa and Grandma. We will fly over the ocean in a big plane. . . .

"Home to you is right here in Germany where you were born, baby darling, but now you are going to learn about another country, a wonderful country, America, that will be your home.

"Your daddy has gone right now to get your papers all fixed, so you can be a real citizen of our United States, little Jamie."

For more than two years Bob Andrews had been in foreign service in Germany. Bob and Anne had been married only two months when they arrived. At first they had kept busy and happy, but when Anne was to have her baby, she became homesick and felt a great need for her own mother. It was almost Christmastime then, too. That was just one year ago. Anne remembered still how lonely and frightened she was then.

"I think when we trust God, he has a way of taking care of mothers and their babies so they won't be too afraid," Bob had comforted her.

Anne smiled now at her baby. Bob was right, she thought, Heavenly Father has been very kind to us.

Suddenly an awful thought crept into Anne's mind. What if. . . . Oh, no, Bob's mother just couldn't expect them to come to her home for Christmas. Anne thought of the big dreary house with its many rooms with everything so somber and untouchable. She had often wondered how a warm, live person like Bob could have grown up in such a place. Anne had never known Bob's father, for he had died several years before her marriage to Bob. Mrs. Andrews lived alone now, and she seemed as solemn and quiet as the old house.

Anne lifted the letter from Mother Andrews. Bob had always said, "You should open Mother's letters, Anne. They are to both of us. Mom would like you to feel like a daughter." For a moment Anne thought she would read this letter to quiet her fears, but she laid it back on the desk unread.

"Don't be silly," Anne told herself. "Of course, Bob's mother will realize that I will want to be with my family for Christmas." She pushed her anxiety aside and began her work again.

Almost every day Anne had told Jamie about her family, about her younger sisters and brothers who would love to play with him. She was determined that he should learn a few words to show off to the family. Bob laughed at her and told her that Jamie didn't understand a bit of the foolishness she tried to tell him.

Only this morning she had been rewarded for her efforts. Jamie said "Gram-ma, Gram-ma." Over and over she had repeated the words to him. Now he laughed and haltingly spoke the syllables. Anne could hardly wait for Bob to come to hear him. She could picture her mother's delight at her first little grandchild speaking those words.

Soon Bob came in flourishing a large envelope. "Now we are all set to leave." . . .

"Oh, and there are letters from our mothers. Mom says they can hardly wait to see us. Won't it be fun showing off our son? And home for Christmas, just think!"

Bob clasped her about the waist and swung her around happily. "Mother is going to like having a grandson around. And you know, Anne, I believe the little guy looks a lot like Dad," Bob spoke thoughtfully.

Again, that anxious feeling crept over Anne, and her hand trembled as she handed Bob his letter. She waited tensely for him to open it. . . .

"I'll go on packing while you read the letter to me," she said.

Anne's face was stricken and her arms fell listlessly to her sides as she heard the words of the letter. "I am planning a fine Christmas this year, Bob, with a tree in the corner of the living room just as we used to have when you were a little fellow. You were married just a little while before you went away, so Anne and I hardly know each other. We need to get acquainted, and now you have a little son; how wonderful. I will count on all of you for Christmas."

Bob raised his eyes to Anne's. The bright happiness was gone from her face. She turned away to hide her tears.

"Anne, dear, of course you expected to go to your family for Christmas. Don't feel bad, Anne, that is where we will go." Bob spoke reassuringly.

"But you heard it—in the letter—you heard your mother say she expects us for Christmas. She is counting on us," Anne replied brokenly. . . .

Anne almost wished that Bob would argue about the situation, that he would say, "Mother is lonely and needs us. I have as much right to go to my mother for Christmas as you to yours." But Bob didn't say anything. He was leaving it for Anne to decide. . . .

Time passed quickly now. Soon they were on their way. . . .

"We will be there soon, Bob. At your mother's, I mean," Anne said. Her voice was low, but she tried to smile.

"Oh, Anne, I can't let you do this. I know how you feel," Bob protested.

"We can't disappoint your mother. You know she expects us. We'll have to do it, and go on in a few days to my family." Anne tried to keep her voice even as she told him.

"You are so sweet to do this, Anne."

Anne thought to herself, I don't feel at all sweet or generous. I feel mean, and still think Bob's mother is selfish and thoughtless. . . .

It was now dusk . . . as they left the cab and came up the walk to the Andrews' house. Bob walked ahead with his son in his arms.

. . . Bob rang the doorbell, and as they waited, Anne took hold of Bob's arm. They heard hurried footsteps in the hall. Anne saw the happiness light the woman's face as she embraced her son and her little grandchild. Anne stood back silently, allowing them time to greet each other. Then Mrs. Andrews came to Anne. She seemed a bit awkward and shy. She kissed Anne on the cheek, but still Anne could not feel a great warmth toward this prim, unfamiliar woman.

As they went into the living room, little Jamie clung tightly to his father's neck.

"He isn't used to strangers much yet," Anne said.

"But he soon gets acquainted," Bob told his mother. . . .

"He is learning to say a few words, Mother," Bob said. "He can say 'Gram-ma.' Here, Anne, he will say it for you. Have him say 'Gram-ma' for Mother."

Anne felt sick with disappointment. She had labored so hard to see that Jamie would say these words for her own dear mother. She had never once thought of Bob's mother being the one to hear him first. She took Jamie in her arms and pointed to Mrs. Andrews. "Say 'Gram-ma,' Jamie. Say 'Gram-ma,' " Anne repeated.

Jamie looked strangely at this woman smiling at him, then began to say over and over, "Gram-ma, Gram-ma, Gram-ma." He was delighted by so much attention.

Bob and his mother laughed together and were very pleased, not noting that Anne stood without even a smile. . . .

"He is tired and excited and should be in bed," Anne said a bit too abruptly.

"Of course he is. I will show you where he will sleep." Bob's mother led the way to the stairs.

Anne, looking at the lovely, mahogany stairway, thought: did a mischievous boy named Bob Andrews ever have fun sliding down this polished banister from his room?

Mrs. Andrews stood back watching as they opened the bedroom door.

"Why, Mother, you have fixed my old room with all my baby things, just as it was when I was a toddler like Jamie." Bob laughed, delightedly. "Would you think that my six-feet-two could have ever been little enough to fit into the crib?" . . .

Early the next morning they heard Mother Andrews moving about the kitchen. "We will have our big dinner on Christmas Eve," she had told them.

All day Anne offered to help, but there didn't seem to be much that Mrs. Andrews hadn't prepared already.

"It looks as though there will be turkey left over for weeks and plum pudding, too, for we are not staying on here to help eat it up," Anne said to Bob.

"I'd better get downtown and see about our reservations to go on after Christmas. Things may be crowded through the holidays," Bob said.

While Bob was gone, Anne offered to set the table for the dinner. She thought of the hustle and bustle there would be at home now. Her father would call all the family into the living room where they would gather about the piano and sing all the Christmas carols, and afterward her father would read the story of Jesus' birth from Luke.

Later, Anne took Jamie out for a stroll to rest him so that he wouldn't be too tired before dinner was over. She wanted him to be awake for the opening of the gifts.

When Anne returned with Jamie, Mother Andrews told her she had already set the table. Anne felt resentful that she was not allowed to help more. Everything seemed to be ready, and Anne wondered why they did not eat.

"It's always been an ironclad rule that we ate dinner at six. I see Mother still hasn't forgotten it," Bob said to Anne.

"I hope there will be no ironclad rules at our house," Anne said.

"The turkey smells so good," Bob hinted. "I speak to do the carving."

Mrs. Andrews seemed a bit restless and kept glancing at the clock.

She is nervous, not being used to company, Anne thought.

The time slipped by, and it was six fifteen, and still they did not eat.

"What is wrong with Mom? She is always so prompt," Bob commented.

Just then they heard the doorbell ring sharply. Bob's mother hurried to the door.

"Surprise—surprise!" Big and little voices called out happily as Anne's family entered the hall.

"Mother—Daddy—all of you. How did you get here?" Tears of happiness ran down Anne's cheeks. After she had greeted her family, she walked quickly to Mother Andrews and kissed her on the cheek. "How wonderful of you," she said.

"I thought it would be nice to be all together," Bob's mother spoke softly.

Anne chided herself. All the time I was thinking her so selfish, but I was the selfish one. I would have left her here all alone for Christmas, thinking only of myself.

"Bob, did you know this all the time?" Anne asked.

"I'm as surprised as you."

"Anne has been wonderful," Mrs. Andrews declared. "I was a bit worried at first that she might think me quite mean to bring her here."

"I was afraid to tell you, Anne, that there were no reservations for train, plane, or bus for at least two weeks," Bob announced.

"Don't worry," Anne's father declared. "We brought the station wagon along. There will be plenty of room for everyone going home."

Mother Andrews stood back, smiling as though she felt

proud of the results of all her maneuvering. She opened the door to the dining room to show the table all set for a large family.

"I wondered this afternoon why Mother Andrews wouldn't let me set the table, but I see it was part of the surprise." Anne placed her arm lovingly around Bob's mother's waist as she spoke.

They all bowed their heads gratefully over the table spread with delicious, steaming food, as Mrs. Andrews asked Anne's father to offer the blessing. Even baby Jamie folded his tiny hands and bowed his head.

The candlelight flickered over the crystal and silver, casting a soft glow all about them. Anne reached for Bob's hand. There is something so warm and close and precious about this new togetherness of our two families, she thought. Then her eyes turned to a picture of Bob's father that hung on the wall. As Anne looked up, all eyes turned toward the picture. . . .

Suddenly, Anne's father spoke. "See little Jamie. He looks like his Grandfather Andrews."

As they all looked, Mrs. Andrews brushed a tear from her cheek as she said, "Wouldn't Grandpa Andrews be proud of the little boy?"

Now Anne spoke. There was a sweet earnestness in her voice. "I think he knows that we are all here together tonight, and he is very near. Don't you think that Christmas extends into eternity, too?"

Relief Society Magazine, November 1960, pp. 739-44. Myrtle M. Dean, who was born in Mancos, Colorado, in 1890, had many articles and stories published in Church magazines. She and her husband, Charles E. Dean, are parents of five children. She died on March 31, 1970. Note: This story is fiction.

Then We Found the Rocking Horse

DEREK DIXON

The house was very quiet. My wife and three teenage daughters had gone to the first of the end-of-year sales in search of clothing bargains. I sat alone in a deep armchair, an unread book on my knees, looking at the snow-covered lawn where we had found the rocking horse fifteen days before. I was rememb_ring those ten hectic days before Christmas when a simple family home evening resolution had opened so many hearts in what had seemed an iron-hearted town.

We had sung, and we had prayed; and then Wendy had said from the pinnacle of her twelve years, "Christmas isn't like it used to be, is it? There used to be a funny feeling around the house, all warm and cozy and safe, but I can't feel it any more." The others chimed in with their remarks, and a pattern began to emerge. Our recent Christmases had failed because of too much eating, too much television watching, too much wrangling over petty things, too many late nights and late risings, and too much concern for self.

And it looked as though the coming Christmas were going to be the same—a spiritual and family failure. The days would pass and again we would have that terrible, dried-out, flat feeling. Was there no way to change the nature of the season in our home? No way to recapture the true spirit of Christmas?

A pause came in the council, and then my wife began to tell us about some young patients at the school for mentally handi-capped children where she worked as a physiotherapist several hours a week. She spoke of emotional deprivation, of uncaring parents, of pinching poverty in many homes, of being forgotten because "they only smash things, don't they?", and of little hands empty at the time of giving. . . .

My wife proposed that we as a family gather toys for those forgotten children at the school. Approval of her suggestion was unanimous.

The following day we put our plan into effect. We ex-plained to our friends about the children at the school and asked them for any little gifts they might care to contribute.

We received one or two stony stares and some half-promises —beyond that, nothing. We had only recently moved to that neighborhood and had scoffed at remarks that the town was a hard town, full of seemingly materialistic, hard-hearted people. Now it seemed to be more than true.

Disappointed at the lack of contributions, we decided that at least we would make a contribution of our own; and so for the next few evenings, after supper was over, we set to making little dolls' beds out of plywood and hardboard, which we then painted in bright glossy paint; my wife supplied miniature mat-tresses and covers. The kitchen began to look like a Lilliputian army supply base! We made six beds in all.

Still nothing from others. Still we asked. Only six days left to Christmas.

On the fifth day we found a rocking horse standing on the back lawn, shimmering in sunshine and frost, his mane worn but triumphant, his eyes wild with the sight of battle, and in his ears the thunder of the captains and the shouting. On the ground beside him stood a cardboard soapbox full of assorted toys. To this day their coming is a mystery to us. And yet it seemed to be a sign, for that very day people began arriving at the front door with gifts for the forgotten children at the school.

One distant neighbor, a single man, lonely and stiff, a man not even invited to contribute, crossed the street to my wife and blurted out:

"Look here, I haven't anything moneywise; but I have been saving little toy motor cars in matchboxes. I get them from the garage. Every time I buy six gallons of petrol they present me with another motor car. I've got twenty altogether. Well, no man has ever asked me to help in something like this, so I'd like to do my bit now. I'll bring the motor cars along to your house tomorrow night and you can be Santa Claus for me."

And he turned away to hide his embarrassment; but when the following evening came, he was there on the step with his twenty motor cars.

An even greater surprise waited at my office. One young man had been reared in London's harsh East End—a man of prejudice and heated temper to whom my attempts to live my religion were a waving flag to a bull. But that day he came to me and said:

"You and I are not great friends—in fact, I wouldn't help you to the end of the street if you had both big toes fractured; but those children at the school are something different. I see their faces every time I close my eyes. Ginny and I were talking about them and wondering how we could help; and we've decided to give the best we have. In my spare moments, I model and paint airplanes. We hang them from the ceiling at home and admire them from time to time, but beyond that they do nothing, so we thought we would give those. And what does it matter if the kids do smash them up playing with them? An hour's pleasure for such a child is well worth the loss of a few models to us."

That very afternoon he produced a large selection of model airplanes.

When I arrived home that evening, my wife and children had similar experiences to relate—of shy strangers and generous enemies—and of friends, too—all of whom were haunted by visions of the empty-handed children; our front room overflowed with their gifts.

The following day the school van called at our home, and the gifts were loaded on board and delivered to the headmistress to distribute to the children. And that was that.

None of those who contributed gifts ever asked for or received recognition or thanks. At the school only the headmistress ever knew from where the gifts had come. The rest was silence.

But as I sit here in the twilight after Christmas, I wonder if the spirit that permeates our home permeates theirs. For we as a family found again in service to others the real spirit of Christmas. The very walls are alive with sweetness and calm.

And as the winter day moves toward its early close, and the cold stars stare down and the snow upon the lawn reflects back the light from my windows, I think upon the true nature of the universe; for from this small miracle at Christmas, I have learned that every act of man reaches out into the universe. Wheels turn, the gears mesh, eternal balances are set in motion, and the earth is changed by the little secrets of kindness that have no significance at all to any earthly historian.

Ensign, December 1973, pp. 20-21. Derek Dixon, who was born in Worcester, England, was baptized in the Church in 1954. He and his wife, the former Brenda Rose Course, have four children. He has held numerous positions in the Church, including branch and district president. The family now resides in the Brighton Branch of the England South Mission.

The Christmas Cards

DOROTHY BOYS KILIAN

Mrs. Alice Colts, rocking idly in the deep-cushioned platform rocker, stared out the front window into the early December twilight. Nowadays she put off lighting the lamp as long as possible; in the deep shadows it was easier to pretend that Harry's chair was not empty. He had been gone over a year, and she knew she ought not to brood; Harry would say she was much too young to waste her time this way.

But she did allow herself this half hour or so at the close of each lonesome day. Besides, she rationalized, it saved electricity, and goodness knows she had to use her funds carefully now.

She stopped rocking as she saw a small boy skid his bicycle to a stop on the snowy walk out front. He vaulted over the low gate and hurried up the path toward the porch.

A newsboy? Mrs. Colts wondered. As she started for the front door, she could hear him whistling bits of "God Rest Ye Merry, Gentlemen." She smiled wistfully. The holidays were a wonderful time for the youngsters!

"Good evening, Ma'am," the ruddy-cheeked boy said cheerfully. "I'm selling Christmas cards. I have just this one box left, and I thought maybe you'd. . . ."

Mrs. Colts couldn't bear to have him go on. "I'm sorry," she interrupted gently. "I'm not sending out any cards this year."

The boy's eyes widened. "Why, I thought everybody sent Christmas cards!"

She could see he was genuinely surprised.

"Well, maybe someday again," she said. "Right now, I'm just not in the mood."

"What will your friends think?" the boy asked.

"Oh, I think they'll understand," she answered lightly. "Now, if you will excuse me, it's pretty cold standing here with the door open. . . ."

"Please, if you could only take this one box!" The boy apparently didn't realize he had been dismissed. "You see," he went on eagerly, "if I sell a dozen boxes I get a bonus and that will give me enough to buy those ice skates for my brother. This is the twelfth box." He held it out toward her.

"Well, you haven't even shown me the cards," Mrs. Colts said, smiling.

"Oh, yes, sure," the boy laughed. He snatched off the lid of the box. "See?" he said proudly. "The newest kind—these long thin ones with modern pictures."

Mrs. Colts, whose tastes ran to old-fashioned snow scenes with green fir trees and red barns, gazed down at a tan deer with an elongated head and pointed ears who stared fixedly at her from a funereal black background. Stifling a groan, she glanced back up at the boy. He was smiling at her, obviously with complete confidence in her good judgment.

"How much?" Mrs. Colts quavered.

"Only a dollar for the box."

"I'll take it."

She put the box of cards away in the desk, thinking that possibly next year she would use them. That is, if she somehow managed to survive this present lonely holiday season. Maybe she should have accepted her son Fred's invitation to come out to Cleveland after all. But he and his wife were living in a tiny apartment and were crowded enough with young Freddy. No, she had made the right decision, painful as it was.

As she started sadly for the kitchen to cook herself a bite of supper, the doorbell rang. Startled, Mrs. Colts turned back to the front of the house.

On the porch stood a little old woman, shoulders bent, with a huge black handbag on her arm. "I don't suppose," the woman said hesitantly, drawing a box from the bag, "that you'd be interested in buying a few cards?"

Mrs. Colts stared at her unbelievingly.

"I know it's pretty late," the woman went on in a tired, thin tone, "but I thought maybe you'd need a few extra at the last minute."

Mrs. Colts found her voice at last. "Why, I bought some from a young boy just a few minutes ago."

The woman didn't seem surprised. She nodded her head sadly. "Yes, your neighbors said somebody else had just been through this street," she said. "Well, thank you anyway." She put the box back in her bag and stepped carefully down the first step of the porch.

Why, she isn't half trying, Mrs. Colts thought. Somehow she felt as irritated as if she were the one who was missing out on a sale.

"Just a minute," she said briskly. "What kind of cards do you have?"

The woman turned back. "Oh, just the usual," she said dispiritedly. "The village church, the skating pond, and such."

"That's just the type most of us older people like," Mrs. Colts said firmly. "Come in for a minute, and we'll have a look at them together." She felt a warm glow as she saw a shadow of hope creep into the faded gray eyes confronting her.

Fifteen minutes later she said goodbye and Merry Christmas to a smiling old Mrs. Ames, and sat down at the desk to reexamine her two new boxes of greeting cards. The old-fashioned scenes brought back a flood of happy memories, and it wasn't long until she had decided it would be nice to send a few cards this year, at least to her dearest friends.

Supper forgotten, she found her address book and set to work. Fortunately, the majority of her friends knew of Harry's passing, so she didn't have to write about that. In most cases she merely wrote on the card "Love, Alice" and popped it into its envelope.

By seven o'clock she had gone through the usual list of folks that she and Harry had sent to in recent years. She still had several cards left, though, and she sat turning them over on the desk. Staring at a picture of a group of carolers under a street lamp, she thought back to the old high school crowd who used to go out singing together on Christmas Eve. And then John would take her home afterwards.

John Roberts was her first beau. She hadn't really thought of him in years. When she'd left Stevensville to take a job in a city office, they had just drifted apart. She had met and married Harry, and she had heard that John had married Vera Higgins, a hometown girl, a couple of years afterwards.

I'll just send them a card, she thought, light-heartedly. No harm done after all these years, and they certainly will be surprised. She addressed a card to Mr. and Mrs. John Roberts, Stevensville, Ohio, but of course, they might have moved away years ago.

Three days later Mrs. Colts arrived home from the post office in the cold dusk of late afternoon and let herself in the front door. All day she had been working against time, finishing the homemade gifts for her son's family. This was the last possible day she could mail the package and be sure of its getting to Cleveland on time. . . .

She took off her wraps and was about to sit down in the chair by the window as usual. Suddenly, perhaps because of the memory of the bustling crowds, the laughing faces, and the festive decorations downtown, she rebelled. "Is this all I'm going to do with the rest of my life?" she asked herself.

Determinedly, she strode over to the table lamp in the front window. As she bent to switch it on, the corner of her eye caught a shadow out by the front gate. A man was standing there, a long box under his arm, one hand on the latch, staring in at the unlighted house. He half opened the gate, then allowed it to swing shut again.

Instantly, Mrs. Colts recognized the symptoms of a reluctant salesman. She took her hand away from the light switch. I can't go through all that again, she thought wildly. Anyway, doesn't the poor fellow realize it's too late to be selling cards?

Then, as she watched, the man slowly took his hand off the gate, pulled up his coat collar, and began to turn away.

"Oh, well," Mrs. Colts sighed resignedly as she switched on the light. "I guess it won't kill me to buy a dollar box for next year."

As the cheerful patch of light fell on the snow-covered front lawn, the man turned back, opened the gate, and started up the path. Before Mrs. Colts left the window, she had time to note that there was something oddly familiar about his stride.

She snapped on the porch light and opened the door. The man was just reaching out to press the bell, but when he saw her he put his hand up to his hat instead, swept it off, and stood there, silver-haired and smiling. "Alice!" he said quietly.

Mrs. Colts stared at him. "John, John Roberts!" she exclaimed at last. "Why, I thought you were. . . ." She laughed and pointed to the box in his hand. "I thought you were another Christmas card salesman. I was just about to be softhearted again and buy some more that I couldn't possibly use."

John Roberts chuckled. "I'm glad, though, you bought those you did, Alice. Otherwise I wouldn't have learned your whereabouts again after all these years. I gathered from the way you signed the card that Harry is. . . ."

"Yes," Mrs. Colts said softly, "over a year ago. It was hard. . . ."

"I know," John said gently. "My Vera, too, three years ago."

They looked at each other with warm compassion.

Then John Roberts squared his shoulders. "If you'll allow me to come in, you can find out what's really in that box." After thirty-five years, his eyes had the same twinkle.

"Of course, John." Mrs. Colts stepped back apologetically. "My goodness, I'm so surprised I've completely forgotten my manners. Come in and take your coat off."

"This is a pleasant room!" John exclaimed, looking around him at the book-lined shelves, the easy chairs, the open hearth, the warm lamplight.

"Yes, it is." Mrs. Colts found herself agreeing heartily. It did seem to have a glow about it that she hadn't been aware of for a long time. "Now, perhaps we could build a little fire in the fireplace—the wood's right here in the basket."

"An excellent idea," John answered. "That was a cold walk up from the depot."

"By the way," Mrs. Colts paused in the door on her way to the kitchen, "you said you'd tell me what was in that box."

John, already on his knees before the fireplace, looked back at her over his shoulder. "Peanut brittle," he said, grinning. "Remember when I was courting you, I used to bring you pounds of the stuff—couldn't afford chocolates."

Mrs. Colts smiled mistily. "Yes, I remember." She started down the hall with a lighter step than had been heard in that house for many a day.

Relief Society Magazine, November 1957, pp. 730-33. Dorothy Boys Kilian, a native of the Midwest, has resided in Pasadena, California, for many years. She has three children. Mrs. Kilian has written extensively and edited a weekly church paper for seventeen years. Note: This story is fiction.

The Christmas Shoppers

LUCILE C. READING

The stores were gay with the glitter of Christmas and filled with exciting games and gadgets, and with warm and appealing clothing to tempt Timmy, age nine, and his seven-year-old brother Billy who, with Mr. Smith, were doing their Christmas shopping.

They had gone from store to store, looking at many possible gifts and then always shaking their heads when a clerk asked if she could help them. Billy had almost bought a game he wanted, and Timmy had paused an unusually long time before a display of books, but after whispered consultation with each other, the boys had decided in each case to look further. Finally impatient, Mr. Smith asked, "Where would you suggest we look next?" He was a member of a club that each year helped to make Christmas happier for poor families. He had given Timmy and Billy each four dollars and had taken them shopping for gifts they especially wanted.

"Could we go to a shoe store, sir?" asked Timmy. "We'd like a pair of shoes for our dad. He hasn't any to wear when he gets better and can go back to work."

When they reached the shoe store, Billy pulled something out of his pocket and handed it to Timmy, who smoothed a crumpled piece of brown paper before giving it to the clerk and explaining it was a pattern of their Dad's foot. They had carefully drawn it while their father slept in a chair one evening. The clerk studied the pattern and then walked away. He returned in a few minutes, held out a box holding a pair of shoes, and asked, "Will these do?"

The shoes were so beautiful that the boys almost held their breath. Then Timmy saw the price on the box. "We only have $8.00," he said, disappointed, "and these shoes are $16.95."

The clerk cleared his throat. "They have been," he answered, "but they're on special today for Christmas gifts. They'll cost you just $3.98, and you'll have money left over for something for yourselves."

"Not for us," the boys exclaimed, "but we can get something for our mother and our two little sisters. Thank you, oh, thank you, sir!"

Over the boys' heads, the clerk and Mr. Smith exchanged meaningful looks. But Timmy and Billy, excited at being able to buy presents for the rest of the family, paid no attention to the men. They could hardly wait to finish their Christmas shopping.

Children's Friend, December 1969, p. 9. Lucile Reading, a native of Logan, Utah, resides in Centerville, Utah. She and her husband, Keith E. Reading, have two sons. Brother Reading died in 1973. Sister Reading has served in the general presidency of the Primary, and is now managing editor of the *Friend*.

The Christmas Gift

KATHRYN E. FRANKS

The moment Danny, my five-year-old, barged into the kitchen and slid onto a chair beside the kitchen table where I was cutting out a red Christmas apron, he asked, "What would you like for Christmas more than anything else?"

I felt certain that the question was connected with something he was making at school. "Oh," I said smiling, "I'd like a new automatic washer, a set of good china, a bright red Christmas dress with some sparkly trimming, a sewing machine, a pancake turner, a wastepaper basket. . . ."

With that Danny suddenly dived under the table. I was cutting again by the time he sneaked back upon the chair. He continued his serious probing. "If you had a new washer," he asked, "what color would you want it to be?"

"Pink," I replied quickly, "to match the new wallpaper."

Sunlight bursting through the kitchen window couldn't have brightened his face more, and something about the answer caused him to pop off the chair and simply cartwheel straight out of the kitchen.

Although Danny didn't mention the subject for several days, it came often to my mind.

I wondered what in the world he might be making that held so much excitement and mystery. No use guessing.

Finally a small clue appeared the evening before the Christmas program.

"I need some wrapping paper for a gift," he reminded me at bedtime. "Will you put a pretty piece out with my school clothes so I won't forget, please?"

I did as he asked, but was informed the next morning that one sheet wasn't enough. "I need two or three sheets," he announced proudly.

Good land, I thought, what would take all that paper?

The next afternoon he brought the gift home in his friend's car and ordered me to hide in the kitchen while he hid it behind his bed. I promised not to peek, and a promise is a promise. Although the dust, shoes, and socks collected, I neither vacuumed or swept behind his bed.

The following day we brought a window-high, wide-branched Christmas tree home and placed it next to the front picture window. With childish excitement we decorated right away. Danny either hung too many ornaments on one limb, causing it to limp down, or not enough on another so that a vast emptiness appeared in another spot. Nevertheless, the branches cast a spruce-like fragrance through the house, bringing the reverence of the season.

The minute we finished, Danny dashed into his bedroom and came out lugging his gift in his still-chubby arms. The gift was so round his arms could barely reach around it.

I held my breath, for it was so flimsily wrapped I felt it was going to appear any second if he didn't stop rearranging it under the tree. First he placed it in front, then he changed it to the back, finally deciding to place it at an angle under an overhanging branch at the side.

"It's so light," I told my husband later that evening, "for anything the size and shape of an old butter crock." But I didn't peek, and I never guessed.

Naturally I was eagerly waiting on Christmas morning when the first thing Danny did was rush over to the tree and grab his gift from under the tree and thrust it into my hands. I tore off the paper and ribbon with gusto. "Look," I exclaimed, holding up the gift for the family to see, "a wastepaper basket. Danny, you fingerpainted this beautiful *pink* carton, didn't you?"

I'm sure my face showed my sincere excitement, for surprisingly enough the hand-painted deer and other designs made a delightfully different basket.

"Do you like it?" Danny asked, forgetting his own gifts under the tree.

"Like it," I said, hugging him. "I love it."

After the gifts were unwrapped he came over to me with a worried look and said, "But, Mother, you didn't get an automatic washer, a sewing machine, or a red dress. Why are you so happy?"

"I'm happy," I answered, holding him from me where I looked at the five-year-old size of him, "because I got a wastepaper basket, a pink, hand-painted one that exactly matches my bathroom walls."

At that he simply cartwheeled over the discarded Christmas wrapping right into the branches of the Christmas tree.

Relief Society Magazine, December 1964, pp. 932-33. Kathryn E. Franks and her husband, who is advertising manager for a California newspaper, have three sons. They live in La Crescenta, California. Note: This story is fiction.

Mama and the Magic Bag

LILA L. SMITH

The howling wind made the tall old house rock and creak. It came down the stovepipe blowing puffs of smoke into the room from the big potbellied stove.

The windows were rattling, and Mama was stuffing rags into the cracks to hold back the snow. I ran to her and held onto her skirt. Sternly she told me to let go so she could move around.

She stopped for a minute, scraped frost from the glass pane, and looked out, then started to cry. Mama cried a lot these cold winter days. Papa said she was just homesick, but I knew better, for I heard them talking after they put me to bed.

"There's no use our staying in this God-forsaken place," Mama said. "Now that you have sold the cattle, we can go back to Southern Utah, and live like other people!"

"I am not leaving the land I took in as part payment on the cattle," Papa said. "Besides, Canada is a coming country; already the land is fast being taken by homesteaders."

I did not know what a God-forsaken place was, or what homesteaders were, but I thought it must have something to do with all the snow and ice piling up outside, and I thought something terrible would happen to us as it did to the people in the Bible when God did not like them.

It was dark when Papa and the boys came in, stomping the snow from their boots and clothes. Mama lit the lamp and started supper.

"Is it time to put the nails in the wall for the stockings?" I asked Mama.

"Yes; get your brothers to put them in behind the kitchen stove, so the things Santa puts in them won't freeze," Mama said, looking at Papa.

"Do you think Santa Claus can get through the deep snow?" I whispered to my big brother.

"Sure," he said. "Mr. Taylor at the post office says he always gets through. Sometimes the mailman brings things for him."

I ran to get the stockings and started hanging them on the nails, but as I reached far over to the last nail my hand slipped and I touched the back of the hot stove. I let out a scream. Papa picked me up and started soothing me.

Mama did not say a word. She just reached for the magic bag from the top of the cupboard, took me from Papa, put salve that smelled of camphor on my burned arm, and wrapped a clean white cloth around it.

She dried my eyes, kissed my cheek, and put me in the big rocker. "You'll be all right now," she said with a smile. "Just think about it being Christmas Eve and Santa coming."

Somehow it did not hurt any longer, and I almost fell asleep as I smelled the loaves of brown bread Mama was taking from the oven and watched her dish up hot stew for our supper.

The house did not creak any longer, and after supper my brothers rubbed the frost off the window so we could see the deep snow glistening in the moonlight.

Papa said the storm was over, and Mama said, "After three days it is about time, or we will all be buried alive!"

We had just settled down to story reading when the knock came at the door.

Papa opened it, and a big man in a fur coat and hat came in. He was covered with snow, and icicles hung from his eyebrows and mustache.

"I am Mr. Armstrong," he said. "My wife needs help, and I

can't get through those drifts to Kimball to get Mrs. Talbot in time. I heard that your wife has had training with the sick, so I came to ask her to help us."

Mr. Armstrong was all out of breath when he had finished. Papa tried to take his coat and hat, but Mr. Armstrong said, "No, there is not time. I must get back."

Mama took down the magic bag, and opened it to check the medicine inside, and then I followed her into the bedroom and watched while she combed her long black hair. She whirled it round and round and then pinned it in a big bob on top of her head. She put on a clean white apron and let me kneel beside her while she said her prayers.

Papa helped her into his big fur coat; he put Lorin's overshoes on her feet. She put a wool fascinator scarf around her head and then followed Mr. Armstrong into the cold, frosty night.

I cried myself to sleep when Papa put me to bed. It was sad not to have Mama home when Santa Claus was coming.

The room was still dark when I woke up and saw the light shining through the curtain over the doorway. I jumped out of bed and ran into the big room that was kitchen, boys' bedroom, and living room for our family.

A blast of cold air came in the door with Mama and Mr. Armstrong. They were both covered with snow. Mama said the horse could not pull them and the buggy through the deep drifts and they had to get out and walk. She looked tired and pale. Papa helped her off with the big coat.

In my excitement at seeing Mama I had forgotten about Santa and the stockings. Then the boys jumped out of bed, and we went to look behind the stove. Santa had got through. The boys had skates, and standing beneath my stocking was a pretty Red Riding Hood doll.

But I lost interest in the doll when I heard Mr. Armstrong say that Mama had given them a beautiful baby boy for Christmas!

The rest of the day I played with my doll but kept looking at the magic bag on top of the cupboard in hopes another Christmas baby would come out.

We ate our dinner of roast beef, mashed potatoes, and creamed carrots, topped off with Mama's suet pudding and sauce, which we could hardly choke down after Mama told us there would be no Christmas dinner at the Armstrongs, just potatoes, cabbage, and an egg, if the hens laid enough. The early snow and freezing had covered their crop before it could be cut and threshed.

After the boys had washed the dishes for Mama, Papa brought around the horses and sleigh to take Mama to see how Mrs. Armstrong and the baby were getting along, and we all went with them.

The horses lunged through the deep snow, sending snowballs from their hooves back into the sleigh. We laughed when the drifts were so high the sleigh bounced over the top, jarring us when it hit bottom.

We arrived at the Armstrong house that looked like two boxes put together with a lean-to porch in between. Papa tied the horses, and we followed Mama into one of the boxes. I looked at the other door, and just knew it must be the stable. The side we went in was a kitchen where four children sat with their coats on, huddled around the stove.

"You better keep your coats on," the oldest boy said. "There's not enough wood to keep both stoves going, and Mama and the baby must be kept warm. Papa has gone over to an old shed to find more wood."

Mama told me to take off my hood and mittens. But when I pulled off my mittens out came the two red apples I had carried clenched in my fists, and they rolled on the floor. I was afraid Mama would scold—but she just smiled as I picked them up and gave them to the two little girls.

Mama took the kettle from the stove and the magic bag and left for the stable. I helped the two girls cut out paper dolls from a catalog, and my two brothers played marbles with the two Armstrong boys.

Papa came in carrying a big box. He took out Mama's big roaster and put it in the oven and then piled wood and a few chunks of coal in the stove.

Soon Mama came to the door and told us we could come see the baby.

When we went through the other door it wasn't a stable, but a big bedroom. The baby was in a cradle made of a wooden box, not a manger. He had a red face, but no halo on his head as it shows the Christmas baby in the Bible stories!

Then we left for home, and the setting sun made the white world and clouds look pink.

Mama said, "This has been a beautiful Christmas day."

And we sang "Jingle Bells" to the sound of the squeaking sleigh runners cutting the crisp snow.

When we arrived home Mama and I took off our wraps, my brother Ray brought in the coal, and Papa built up a warm fire.

"What's for supper, Mama?" Lorin asked.

"Oh, we can make sandwiches from the roast beef left from dinner," she said.

"I don't think we can," Papa said. "I took it and the gravy to the Armstrongs. But we can have the rest of the suet pudding and sauce."

"No, we can't," Mama said. "I took that to Mrs. Armstrong."

"Well, boys, let's have some of the nuts and candy from your stockings," Papa said, "because it won't matter if they do spoil our appetites now."

"We can't give you any from our stockings, Papa, we took them to the Armstrong children," Ray said.

Everyone laughed, and we made jokes and riddles while we ate our supper of bread and milk.

From then on if anything was lost, we would ask, "Did you take it to the Armstrongs?"

Mama never cried by the window any longer; she was too busy making carbolic salve, camphorated oil, liniment, and canker medicine from the recipes Grandpa Pugh had brought across the plains with him in the magic bag. They had been given to him by his Welsh ancestors and given to Mama when she left for Canada.

Mama always said she found a magic recipe for happiness in the magic bag that Christmas Eve, and she often told it to us: A lot of faith, with a lot of work, will make everything turn out right. And never feel sorry for yourself—there is always someone in the world with more miseries than your own.

All winter she went through blizzards, rain, winds, and floods to help children with croup, pneumonia, and broken bones. She left babies for ranch women, women on lonely homesteads, and women across the boundary line on the Indian reservation.

Through it all she had a smile, time to tell us stories, and time to sing.

Relief Society Magazine, December 1969, pp. 894-97. Note: This story is fiction.

The First Christmas Greeting

LOUISE D. MORRISON

Time to shut up shop, Will," said Mr. Broadbent to his apprentice in his engraving shop in England more than one hundred years ago.

"Come along. Tomorrow's Christmas Day." Mr. Broadbent was chuckling as he rolled down his sleeves and slipped on his coat. "I'm off to buy a goose for our dinner. Won't we be living grand?"

"Yes," Will said slowly, pulling on the coat which Mrs. Broadbent had kindly mended for him. "I wish—oh, Mr. Broadbent, you're the best man a boy could be apprenticed to, and I do wish I had some money to buy presents for you and Mrs. Broadbent and Elizabeth."

"Don't worry, lad." Mr. Broadbent gave him a friendly pat on the shoulder. "Gifts don't matter. It's not what you have in this world. It's how we feel about one another that counts."

"I suppose," Will agreed ruefully. "My father wrote he was sending me money, but it hasn't come."

"In weather like this?" Mr. Broadbent gave a jolly laugh. "You expect horses to have wings to get through the snowy roads this time of year? Your father's off in Scotland painting miniatures of grand ladies and gentlemen, and the money will get here as soon as it can."

The wind whistled as Mr. Broadbent opened the door to the shop and the two of them went out into the fog. "Run along home and tell Mrs. Broadbent I shall be a bit late. Getting the goose, you know."

Cold snow bit Will's thin, gentle face. He hunched his shoulders and hurried along the narrow streets, looking up occasionally as a carriage with fine horses passed. If only he could give the Broadbents something for Christmas. . . .

"Come to the fire, lad." Mrs. Broadbent wiped her hands on a wide expanse of patched apron. "Warm up a bit."

After Mr. Broadbent returned home triumphantly with the goose, they all had some tasty soup, swept the hearth, and put some chestnuts to roast on the fire. They sang "God Rest Ye Merry, Gentlemen" and "Silent Night" before they blew out the candles for the night.

Slowly, Will went to his room, his Christmas spirit almost sapped by the unhappy thought that he had nothing to give. He sat in the chilly room, his candle flaring on the table, and looked about him at his worldly possessions—his clothing, a miniature of his dead mother, which his father had done in delicate pastel shades, and the paints his father had given him. Like his father, Will had early shown a talent in art, and he was the proudest fellow for miles around when his father presented him with some art materials.

For Will the most treasured gift in the world was a picture.

Gift? Gift! Suddenly the boy stood up straight, fired with an idea. A picture! He would paint a picture for the Broadbents for Christmas.

Excitement made his cold hands tremble a little as he arranged his materials and began to work.

The next morning when he heard the merry calls of the family on Christmas Day, Will hurried out of bed and took his picture down, presenting it to Mr. Broadbent apologetically. "It's not much, but here's a Christmas greeting for the family."

They all admired the picture of a family gathered around a heavily laden dinner table. On one side was a group of carolers and on the other a skating scene, all done in the reds and greens of the holiday season. Under the three panels so typical of the holiday in England, he had written in large letters: "A Merry Christmas and a Happy New Year."

"That's the most Christmassy present I've ever seen," said Elizabeth.

"Indeed it is," Mr. Broadbent chuckled. "What a pity more people don't receive greetings from their friends at Christmastime."

"I guess people wouldn't have time to make very many each year," Will said.

Then the boy found Mr. Broadbent looking at him in a strange and serious way. "Come, come, lad!" he said. "They can be lithographed."

And so they were. The next year, 1842, William Egley made up a sketch which was lithographed and filled in with colors.

So, from the deep desire in a boy's heart to give greetings to friends at Christmastime, arose the custom we have today of exchanging Christmas cards.

Children's Friend, December 1961, pp. 40-42. Louise D. Morrison, a native of Nashville, Tennessee, is on the faculty of the Case Western Reserve University in Cleveland, Ohio. She and her husband, Thompson Morrison, have one daughter.

The Fiftieth Cake

IVY W. STONE

Jeanette Parsons, famed as a maker of wedding cakes, stood at her white enamel kitchen table, the ingredients of a cake spread out before her in methodical array. The glass mixing bowl held butter and sugar. Citron and orange peel, pineapple, and cherries were ready for the chopper. Egg whites in one bowl, yolks in another. Nuts ready to be cracked, raisins and currants to be cleaned, dates and prunes to be pitted. The red spice boxes stood in a neat row; the soda and baking powder were measured. The linoleum glistened from a recent scrubbing in milk; the range shone from its polish of paraffin. The Christmas cactus gave promise of blooms in season, while the chintz curtains and Jeanette's apron vied for supremacy in whiteness.

Miss Parsons' blue-black eyes were Scotch; her brown, curly hair was Irish. But the curls were combed into a prim, tight knot, and the eyes were drawn into a pucker. Miss Parsons looked her thirty-five years.

"One, two, three, four," she counted as she measured cups of flour into the sieve. Making a wedding cake in the solitude of her own kitchen was a simple matter to the experienced Jeanette, but having to entertain the prospective bride and listen to her endless questions and chatter was nearly calamitous.

"Why didn't you ever marry, Miss Parsons?" From across the table Cherry Barton, soon to become Mrs. Kenneth J. Merrick, put her question with no thought of hesitancy.

"Six, seven, eight," Jeanette continued to count, and bent farther over the flour bin. Only a quick flush up her neck revealed she had heard Cherry's lightly put question.

"You missed five, Miss Parsons. You've only got seven cups."

"I declare, Cherry," Jeanette's voice indicated forced patience, "when I agreed to make your wedding cake, I never expected to have to entertain you while I made it. Now I'll have to measure that flour all over again. You keep still, Cherry, till I'm through counting."

Thus rebuked, Cherry rinsed the raisins under the tap with a quick splash and spread them out on a pie tin. "There," she announced triumphantly. "Your raisins are washed."

"Did you pick 'em over?"

"Did I what?" Cherry looked puzzled.

"Did you sort 'em? They're labeled 'cleaned and ready for use,' but it isn't so. Little, tiny stems are buried in the meats, and seeds pop up like mushrooms. I ain't intending your husband's folks from Boston are going to find seeds and stems in the cake that I baked." . . .

"I'd much rather you put the old cake away and told me of your blighted romance," persisted Cherry. "Something's happened, I know, to keep you single. Your saucy blue eyes and brown curls have a come-hither look."

"I'd much rather you'd go home and let me finish this cake before I spoil it," retorted Jeanette with the familiarity of old friends. "If your mother wasn't such a real friend, I'd never have done it so near Christmas. . . . There child, don't worry," she consoled, patting her shoulder. "If you'll just sit and watch, you can stay all day. Brides are that way; can't settle to do anything. Everybody working for them, too. With your wedding only four days off, your eyes shouldn't be red. . . ."

"If you had ever let a man see you bake a cake, Miss Jeanette, I'm sure you would be married. It's marvelous. It's a poem. No wonder you get seventy-five cents a pound. It's worth a dollar."

"December butter and eggs are expensive." Jeanette pushed the stiff batter high into the corners and left it low in the center of each pan.

"Why?" queried Cherry, intensely interested.

"So it'll rise level. I don't never have lopsided cakes. They don't look nice. A lopsided cake is the mark of a poor cook."

The pans were placed in the oven with slow, careful precision. Miss Parsons shut the door cautiously, examined the fire, marked the hour of the clock, and turned to her guest.

"We'll sit a spell before we wash up the dishes. I never jiggle the floor for half an hour."

"Why didn't you marry?" The irrepressible Cherry reached for the batter spoon and knocked over an open box of nutmeg. "I'm so happy, and Ken is so grand. I hate to think of you living here alone. On winter nights and holidays, it must be dreadful lonesome."

"This is my forty-ninth cake, and forty-eight other brides have asked the same question. Brides get romantic, Cherry. They want everybody else to get into the same boat. They can't rest till they pair everyone off. I never told the others. It wasn't their business. But your mother knows, and you would wiggle it out of her. I ain't married because I won't light a red lantern and stick it in my window." Miss Jeanette pointed to an upper shelf where a red-globed lantern occupied a place of prominence.

"I have the match to light it, too," continued Miss Jeanette, keeping a practiced eye on the clock. "But I'm Irish stubborn, and I won't, somehow I can't, bring myself to be so bold as to send a man a signal I want him. He knows where I live. Let him come when he wants me." Her mouth set in lines that were too firm for beauty. "This is my forty-ninth cake. I'm baking only one more wedding cake for other folks. When you change from a girl to a woman, baking cakes for other brides, fifty is about enough. I'll bake just one more." She folded her hands and set her chin in a manner that suggested pioneering ancestors.

"Is it ordered?" Cherry's eyes danced with sudden inspiration. "Have you already promised to make that last cake?"

"No, and I'm glad I haven't. Christmastime is too busy for

extras like weddings. I hope nobody orders a cake till folks can settle down to normal again. You can't make a pretty cake when it has to be flat and cut into samples and put in satin boxes, like this of yours. I used to make them three tiers high. I used a six-quart pan for the bottom, a four-quart for the middle, and a one-quart for the top. I decorated them with roses and wreaths and put a little bride and groom on the top. Them was cakes. Nowadays, young folks get married at the courthouse and hustle off, with no reception or old shoes or rice. Somehow they don't seem like weddings at all."

"Miss Jeanette," in her eagerness, Cherry put her elbow into the batter spoon, "do you mean, honest, if you lit that lantern you'd get a husband? It sounds like the Arabian Nights, where the boy rubbed the magic lamp. A match to a wick, and presto! A bride!"

Miss Jeanette smiled, but with a grim, stubborn, "I-won't-give-in" expression.

"If I set that lighted lantern in my window tonight, I'd have a would-be-husband in an hour."

"Let's do it!" cried the undaunted Cherry. "We could have a double wedding. . . . Now! Please!"

"I guess not!" Forgetting the wiggly floor, Jeanette rose to her full height and looked so stern that Cherry subsided. "I don't send for any man because I need him. That I might want him is a different matter. If he wants me, let him come here.

"You see, Cherry, it was before Father died, when you were a little girl. We got to going out together, and we'd have been married all right, but Father got dreadful sick and took a terrible dislike to Martin. He was unreasonable. Wouldn't say why he didn't like him. Just told him to go and never come back. I fancy he was afraid Martin would take me away from him, when he needed me so. Father was so sick you couldn't argue with him, so Martin left. He was proud, too. He never forgot the things Father said to him. He never come back till Father died. After the funeral, he come to see me, and he brought two lanterns with red globes. He says: 'Jeanette, here are two lanterns with red globes. You keep one and I'll keep one. It's too soon after your sorrow to talk of marriage, but when you need me, put your lantern in your window, and I'll come. If I need you, I'll light mine.' That was seven years ago."

"And you never sent for him?" Cherry was incredulous. "I'd have brought Ken back the next night."

"I take it down to clean the shelf, and I put it back. Once I changed the oil."

"And you eat alone three times a day," cried Cherry, to whom solitude would mean death. "And you go out and work for other folks and make your own fires and carry your own coal. Oh, it's too foolishly proud. You silly old dears. What does he do?"

"He gardens and lives alone and pretends to keep house after work. His washings look scandalous. . . ."

"Both of you come home late at night to cold, cheerless houses. . . . Aren't you ever going to light that lantern?"

"He said, 'When you need me, I'll come.' So long as the good Lord gives me health and work to do, I don't need a man," persisted the Irish-Scottish combination. Her lips set in such a hard, straight line that even the romantic Cherry knew why the Irish-Scottish pioneers conquered the wilderness. They couldn't be driven; they never admitted defeat. Could they be outwitted?

"I'll only make one more," persisted Miss Jeanette, "and I hope it ain't ordered flat like this one."

Mr. Martin Ladd, gardener for the big hospital, knew the ways of plants, but not of women. It never occurred to Martin Ladd that marriage was a matter of love and not necessity. So Martin Ladd awaited Jeanette's summons to return. Until Jeanette sent for him, as he had told her to do, Martin Ladd lived alone.

The Barton-Merrick society wedding was a huge success. A palm bower hid the orchestra, and all agreed the bride was the loveliest, and her veil the longest of the season. The tiny boxes, containing Miss Parsons' famed wedding cake, created a sensation. Maidens saved them to tuck under pillows. Men said the samples were good and asked for real slices.

Mr. Kenneth J. Merrick was an indulgent husband. He was earnestly anxious to grant any reasonable request his wife might make. But this sudden determination of hers to revisit Mr. Martin Ladd, the bachelor-gardener, seemed rather absurd. Especially on their own wedding night.

"You see, dear," he expostulated, "you and I are so newly married, it seems wonderful. It's hard for us to imagine any happiness except in marriage. But really, they're both old enough to know their own minds. Matchmakers never get thanked."

Young Mr. Merrick sighed and capitulated.

Two days before Christmas, Jeanette Parsons received a telegram. Paid. Needing no answer. Her fingers trembled as she signed the receipt and tore the yellow envelope. Since the tense days of World War I, few messengers found their way to her quiet street.

"Well, of all the nonsense!" she ejaculated after a first hurried reading. "That rattle-brained youngster. Marriage ain't calmed her down one bit." The telegram read:

A friend of Mr. Merrick's has ordered your fiftieth cake. Make it in tiers with wreaths and roses and bride and groom. Price no object. Wedding Christmas Eve.

Cherry.

"I'll do nothing of the sort!" Jeanette spoke to her canary, for lack of a better audience. "This will be one whim of Cherry Barton's which ain't going to be gratified. I've no time to bake cakes." But even as she spoke she went to her pantry. "There's plenty of butter and pineapple, but I'll need raisins and eggs. Wonder who it is that's got sense enough to order a real old-fashioned wedding cake."

Mrs. Barton sent her chauffeur for the cake early in the evening. But he knew nothing of the sudden order for wedding cake. All he could do was hand over a generous check, and the mystery of the cake remained unexplained. Somehow, Miss Jeanette felt loath to part with this last cake. It seemed like a part of herself, leaving the little house forever.

She snapped off her light and raised her north blind. Following the custom of seven years, she glanced toward Martin Ladd's home, two blocks away. Sometimes she had seen a yellow gleam, but more often a black blur, for Martin retired early. Tonight a steady red flame glowed in his window.

"Humph!" sniffed Jeanette, angered at the quickening of her heartbeat. "Just some of them auto lovers. Wonder they don't freeze. So busy courting, they forgot to turn off their rear light." She hurried into bed, turned her back to the red beacon, and counted to one hundred. Not by fives and tens, but in the slow methodical manner she used in counting the cups of flour.

When her Irish heart had succeeded in overcoming her Scottish stubborness, she turned again to the fascinating glow. It was still there. Martin's signal of distress. After seven years, he had found need for the waiting woman. Thank heaven the long duress was ended. He was ill, of course. . . . With hands that trembled, she lit her own lantern and watched the long disused wick splutter and flicker before spreading to a steady flame. In her excitement, she donned a short-sleeved, V-necked dress that she seldom wore. She would carry the lantern to guide her way. She could not spare time to follow the sidewalk around the block. Her galoshes, coat, and lantern, and she was ready.

Martin needed her; she must hurry. Across lots was quicker; the irrigation canal had a little bridge, which the lantern would locate for her. The wide cornfield held no menace. Perhaps Martin had pneumonia. He used to have a troublesome cough. He didn't take proper care of himself. Men who lived alone seldom did. The snow was deep, and there was no trace of a path. Only the red glow of the lantern to guide her. . . .

She stumbled up to Martin Ladd's kitchen door. Every blind was tightly drawn. The lantern between the blind and window was the only sign of occupancy.

Jeanette rapped sharply and called, "Martin! Martin, open the door!" Receiving no answer, she boldly turned the knob and walked in. . . . She stepped into the presence of Mr. and Mrs. Kenneth J. Merrick, the county clerk and his wife, and Martin Ladd.

Not a sick Martin. In fact, a very radiant Martin, dressed in his best. A Martin that smiled his love, extended his arms unashamed.

"Jeanie, my dear, I more than need you; I love you." The stubborn reserve withered before his warm smile, and Jeanette accepted his embrace as her just due. . . .

"We're being married right now," he whispered, "with Ken and Cherry as witnesses."

In the curtainless room Miss Jeanette Parsons became Mrs. Martin Ladd. "For richer, for poorer; for better, for worse; throughout our lives." The solemn tones of the clerk's voice filled the little room.

Cherry opened the door to Martin's one best room. There stood the last cake, the fiftieth cake, the center of a sumptuous wedding feast. The frosting was uncracked; the bride and groom still wore their unalterable smiles.

At midnight, Mr. and Mrs. Martin Ladd were left alone. As they stood at the door, bidding their guests good night, the bells began to herald the glorious anniversary.

"Peace on earth, good will to men!"

Relief Society Magazine, December 1932, pp. 693-700. Ivy Williams Stone, who has written many short stories, poems, travelogues, and serials, resides in Alhambra, California. She and her husband, Spencer Stone, who passed away in 1950, are parents of seven children, three of whom are living. Note: This story is fiction.

Photo by H. Armstrong Roberts

To Me It Is One Thing—Joy

BERTA HUISH CHRISTENSEN

hy do some people speak of Christmas as a season of paradox?" Mada asked, thumbing through a sheaf of Christmas carols. "I see nothing paradoxical about it. To me it is one thing—joy."

"One doesn't often hear that statement," I said, "but my father often discussed Christmas in depth and I remember him once actually using that exact term."

"He did? We never even discussed Christmas. We just lived it. At our house the entire holiday was and still is one joyous season. We just socialize, I guess you would say. Relatives call—and stay for dinner. Friends get invited. That's it—a socializing season."

"It certainly should be a joyous season," I said, "but didn't you ever discuss how and what makes Christmas meaningful?"

"Not that I remember, not really. I'm interested in your family discussions and in what your father said, especially."

"Well, Father used to say that Christmas is like the two-faced Janus of Roman mythology. You know—two faces viewing the world in opposite directions, or perhaps viewing past and future time."

"I certainly never heard of such an idea being applied to Christmas. How come?"

"Father really didn't mean to attach Janus to Christmas in a concrete way. He merely meant that there's more to Christmas than one ordinarily sees with two eyes. Father liked to philosophize, and he had quite a lecture on the subject, to some visiting relatives. It isn't very brief. Still want to hear it?"

Mada did, so I began to quote Father as nearly as I could remember his words:

" 'In the daily struggle for survival, it's pretty easy to become a victim of routine and to lose our sense of proportion. We get all tangled up in self-interest. We may consider ourselves generally responsive to the woes of the world, but we don't do much about the neighbor or the friendless family living on the other side of town. The potential for important accomplishment which is in each of us just lies inactive until stimulated by some specific circumstance.

" 'Well, Christmas can be and often is that circumstance. It affects the personality very much like spring changes the winter landscape. We are motivated to forget ourselves, to think of others, and to do kind things for them. This kindness warms us inside, makes us feel so good we wonder why we don't do it oftener. In fact, we are so gratified by the appreciation of those we help that we get to thinking about love and charity and about ourselves, what we do and what we don't do that we should.

" 'We recall the letter we didn't write, the help we didn't give, the friend in the hospital we did not visit, and the opportunity for some special service postponed until too late. We may even express need for an increase of faith.

" 'But repentance is more than admission of neglect and remembering error. It means replacing past performance with wiser, more kindly living. Repentance makes us decide to change our pattern of life. In fact, we resolve to do so, right now. This repentance gives us a peaceful feeling inside. In fact, it's a wonderful feeling. And a sort of spiritual vigor follows the resolve to live differently.' "

I paused here to see if Mada was still with me. The contemplative expression on her face matched her words—"This is certainly a new angle on the Christmas theme. What else did your father say?"

I went on, "Well, Father said, 'The Christmas season is a sort of paradox. On one hand there is happiness, lighthearted enjoyment, carefree sociability, which is as it should be. On the other hand, there is a seriousness, as we appraise the meaning of the Christmas message, and how Christ fits into it. Not so much the manner of his birth as the matter of his life. We appraise ourselves in relation to it, and to those around us, the people we love and those we don't. Serious? Yes, but really warp and woof of the Christmas message. That's the way I see it,' Father said."

Berta Huish Christensen, *Christmas Is for You* (Salt Lake City: Deseret Book Co., 1968), pp. 29-31.

Index